THE NEW
TRAILSIDE
COOKBOOK

THE NEW
TRAILSIDE
COOKBOOK

100 DELICIOUS RECIPES
FOR THE CAMP CHEF

KEVIN CALLAN & MARGARET HOWARD

FIREFLY BOOKS

A FIREFLY BOOK

Published by Firefly Books Ltd. 2013

First Printing

The publisher gratefully acknowledges the financial support for our publishing program by the Government of Canada through the Canada Book Fund as administered by the Department of Canadian Heritage.

Publisher Cataloging-in-Publication Data (U.S.)
Callan, Kevin.
    The new trailside cookbook : 100 delicious recipes for the camp chef / Kevin Callan ; Margaret Howard.
[192] p. : col. photos. ;   cm.
Includes index.
ISBN-13: 978-1-77085-189-4 (pbk.)
1. Outdoor cooking. I. Howard, Margaret. II. Title.
641.578 dc23   TX823.C344   2013

Library and Archives Canada Cataloguing in Publication
Callan, Kevin
    The new trailside cookbook : 100 delicious recipes for the camp chef / Kevin Callan, Margaret Howard.
Includes index.
ISBN 978-1-77085-189-4
1. Outdoor cooking. 2. Cookbooks. I. Howard, Margaret, 1930-
II. Title.
TX823.C25 2013   641.5'782   C2012-906746-6

Published in the United States by   Published in Canada by
Firefly Books (U.S.) Inc.   Firefly Books Ltd.
P.O. Box 1338, Ellicott Station   50 Staples Avenue, Unit 1
Buffalo, New York 14205   Richmond Hill, Ontario L4B 0A7

Cover and interior design: Christine Rae

Printed in China

> ◍ This symbol indicates the
>   ingredient can be brought to
>   camp dehydrated, if necessary
>   (see Chapter 6).

Table of Contents

Introduction

I once went through a stage in my camping life during which I would simply throw bland meals like macaroni and cheese or those prepackaged freeze-dried meals together and head out into the woods to endure a night or two. It certainly didn't last long. I quickly got bored with roughing it out there, and I definitely got tired of eating bad meals.

I devoted more time to trip planning and actually became obsessed with food. Each meal was nutritious and, more importantly, tasty. I bought myself a food dehydrator, which literally changed my life. I was able to go out for longer periods. I flourished out there and loved every minute of it.

Getting meals ready for your camping trip can be overwhelming at times. There are the countless recipes to choose from, the ingredients to pick up, the taste-testing to be done, food to dehydrate if you're heading to the interior or, if you're simply heading to the campground, the perfect cooler to purchase. Then you have to pack it all. It's not hard to fill a minivan, and people choosing to rough it in the wilderness have to stuff everything into packs strapped to their backs. It's a daunting task to say the least.

But then you go on your trip and have the time of your life. Loons serenade in the evening, the kids swim at the beach all day and every meal you prepare works out even better than planned.

The truth is, it's all worth it in the end. You just have to remind yourself of that while running around, packing and preparing everything. So make sure you have fun while preparing for the trip. Try a different recipe, add a secret ingredient, have the rest of the group get involved, organize a pre-trip dinner party — whatever it takes. Remember, it will all be worth it when you get there, and sometimes preparing for a camping trip can be more fun than the actual trip itself.

That's why when my publisher asked if I wanted to coauthor a gourmet camp cookbook, I jumped at the chance. Especially when he told me that the other writer would be Margaret Howard, a former dietitian, food and nutrition consultant and author of over 16 cookbooks. With Margaret making up the recipes and me writing up all the technical how-to jargon, it was a perfect match — like Red Green and Julia Child.

—*Kevin Callan*

I am not an interior camper, but I love writing cookbooks, and working with camping enthusiast Kevin Callan has been very special as he provided me with a great appreciation and knowledge for his beloved activity. His enthusiasm for camping has been quite infectious.

When I say I am not a camper that is not quite true, as our family sailed for many years starting in a 16-foot dinghy before finally moving to a 24-foot sailboat. During those years, we lived on these boats over weekends as well as for longer periods of time as we sailed around Lake Ontario. Much like camping in many respects, the water supply was limited, the cooling methods were less than desirable, and after the ice melted, we resorted to the types of food that an interior camper does. During those years when we sailed in Canada and in the Caribbean our supply of fresh foods was limited by how much cooler storage capacity we had until we arrived at the next port. I recall how we always purchased an entire stalk of bananas (more than 50 on the stalk) and how many bananas we had to eat as they ripened.

Our other family holidays in summer, which included four children and a large and hungry collie, were to a northern cottage. Here, again, the facilities were quite simple, meaning outhouses as well as cooking on a two-burner hot plate, and a wood stove used for warmth when needed, but which was the last thing we wanted to use for cooking on very hot summer days.

My enthusiasm for cooking and for writing cookbooks has never diminished over the 30-plus years and 16 cookbooks I have had the privilege to write for both Canadian and U.S. consumers. From books for product promotion while in the corporate world, to those for healthy eating, to those for people with health concerns such as diabetes, and to fun-loving books on preserving as well as grilling, I have tested, tasted and tested again to ensure all recipes I have written will be fail-proof to the reader. And so to the camp chef, bon appétit!

— *Margaret Howard*

How to Be the Ultimate Camp Chef

The best part of planning a trip is organizing the food. Problem is, if you mess up the trip is guaranteed to fail. But if it's done correctly, the trip will not only be a success, you'll be the top camper in the group for years to come.

Morning Starts

Make sure breakfast is nutritious. It's true what your mother always told you, breakfast is the most important meal of the day. But also keep it quick and simple. Lingering around the campsite in the morning waiting for breakfast to be cooked is a waste of good travel time. The best time to be wandering around in the woods or paddling a lake is early morning. Simple fare like hot or cold cereal or granola with fruit

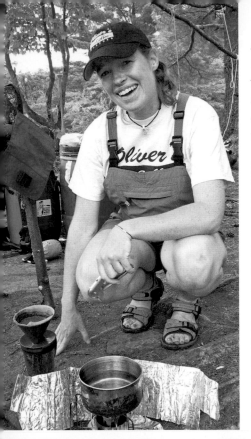

and nuts is a good choice. Pancakes, crepes or bannock is okay if the cook starts cooking while the coffee is being poured. Keep the bacon and eggs for a lazy morning hanging around camp due to bad weather or when boating, and weather has you sitting at anchor.

Midday Meals

Stopping for lunch is essential to a good trip, but taking time out to cook something is a rarity; it's mostly made up of simple things like bannock with PB & J or cheese and crackers. Fancier foods can definitely be served, however, such as couscous salads or cabbage salads. Leftovers from the previous night's dinner can also make a perfect lunch. A portable camp stove can be used to heat up water for soup and hot drinks when the weather is cool and rainy. Better yet, a thermos can be filled with hot water in the morning and used for hot drinks at lunchtime.

Quick Pickups

Snacks are the lifeblood of any good trip. Even if you eat three solid meals a day, snacking can boost morale — and boost your body. The first ever high-energy trail snack was created by the Greek army. In 150 BCE supply officer Philon of Byzantium made up pellets that were a mix of sesame honey (for protein and carbohydrate), opium poppy (to control hunger pains) and a medicinal root called squill (which acted as a stimulant). It probably tasted horrible but did the trick. GORP is today's common high-energy trail snack. GORP stands for Good Old Raisins and Peanuts, but everything goes — salty, crunchy, sweet or chewy. Try adding candy-coated chocolates, beer nuts, dried cranberries, dried mango, banana chips, mini marshmallows, salted pumpkin seeds, corn nuts, mini pretzels, chocolate-covered coffee beans, Grape-Nuts cereal, dried and spiced snow peas, or even dried jalapeño peppers. However you make it though, it's crucial that the GORP eating etiquette is followed: no "high grading" allowed. No one picks and chooses only the bits and pieces they like. Everyone must blindly grab a handful of the entire mixture and munch away. To quote Bill Mason from his book *Song of the Paddle*, "The best way to control high-grading is to pretend you're being polite, grab the bag and give it a good shake as you hold it out. (But don't let go!) Then watch the pained expression as he or she comes up with just a handful of peanuts and raisins."

Dinner

Dinner makes up a good part of the camping trip's entertainment. It's basically social hour, when everyone is in a relaxed pace after a long day. Serving a hearty and nutritious meal is important — just like breakfast — but it's also important to make something fancy. When it comes to food on camping trips, I've seen two main types of food critics. There are the survivalists who just eat to fuel up, caring little for taste. They stuff down boiled noodles and fill in the gaps with energy bars. Good luck to them if they happen to be out for more than a few days. They're sure to crash. Then there are the campers who live to eat. They take great pleasure in outdoing

Make sure to add a garnish to your main meal. A dinner topped with dried parsley or cilantro or, better yet, pine nuts, almonds or peel from a lemon will separate you from the run-of-the-mill camp cooks and guarantee your reputation as a gourmet camp chef.

someone else's recipe and would far rather plan and prepare their own meals than purchase prepackaged camp food. To them, a long trip is a welcome challenge, not something to endure until you get back to the world of fast food restaurants. The fancier the recipes the more positive the group will be — the more glamorous the better. The main ingredient can consist of regular fare, usually pasta or rice, but with a nice sauce and an even fancier name given to it. Make the main meal an extravagant affair and it's a guarantee dinnertime will be one of the highlights of the trip.

And adding that Sweet Ending dessert will make you an even more popular chef.

Timing Is Everything

If you're using a camp stove, then dinner should only take a maximum of 30 minutes to cook to conserve fuel. Even if you're cooking on a campfire, it shouldn't take any longer. Hungry campers get cranky quickly. If the meal does require a little more preparation time then plan on serving appetizers. This will keep everyone's hunger at bay for a while and allow you to concentrate on cooking the main dish. One of the worst feelings in the world is to have other campers gather around you while you're cooking up a meal, standing there and adding their two cents on how things should be done.

Ultimate Camp Cook-off:

To spice up dinner, suggest a friendly camp cook-off competition for the first night out and the last night out. Start by placing everyone in small cooking groups. Choose a judge, who agrees to sample everyone's meal and also agrees not to accept any bribes (this is vital). And you guessed it; the last night's meal is definitely more challenging. Food isn't fresh and recipes are more of the trial-and-error type.

Prizes then must be awarded to the winning group and a major punishment handed out to the losing group, both for the first night and the last night. For example, in my regular group of campers, our first meal motivation is that the cooks of the worst dinner have to do the dishes for the remainder of the trip, and the losers for the last meal have to hand over their remaining spirits (rum, scotch, vodka…) to the rest of the group. Sound serious? It is. But boy have we made some darn good meals because of it.

Shopping & Packing

Bulk food stores are just made for campers. There you'll find all the ingredients necessary to make delicious meals and the prices are always cheaper than in supermarkets.

Here are some of the basic items you can pick up at any bulk food store.

LENTILS: Lentils come in a variety of colors (red, yellow, green or brown) and any can be used; just make sure they're split and de-husked to reduce cooking time, which saves on fuel.

RICE: There is an endless assortment of rices that can be used in many different recipes. Precooked white rice (such as Minute Rice) is less nutritious, but it saves a lot of boiling time and fuel consumption. Mixing rice with lentils is a good idea. Served together, they become a complete protein.

PASTA: All kinds of pastas are available but I recommend whole-grain or flavored vegetable pastas.

BEANS: Dried beans really add to a meal and there are countless varieties. To reduce cooking time, it is crucial that they are presoaked well before mealtime. Place them in a sealed container and let them soak in water at least 8 hours before using them. If you plan on using beans for an evening meal, make sure to place them in a sealed zipper storage bag stuffed in your cook set or a small plastic drinking bottle in the morning. To cook for dinner, drain off the soaking water, add fresh water and depending on the type of bean you are using, the boiling time will have dropped from 2 hours to 20 minutes or a bit longer.

TVP: Textured vegetable protein is a commercially dried soy product used regularly by vegetarians as a meat substitute. It comes in granular or cubed form and is easily rehydrated.

SOY GRITS: For a quick, high-protein dinner, try soy grits. They're similar to soy flour except the soybeans have been toasted and cracked into tiny flakes rather than ground into a powder.

BULGUR: Bulgur is a processed form of wheat kernels that have been steam cooked and dried. It has a nutlike flavor, which makes it a good breakfast, but it is also an excellent substitute in any recipe calling for ground beef.

TOASTED BUCKWHEAT: Buckwheat is a seed produced by a grasslike herb and is high in potassium and phosphorus.

HARD WHEAT KERNELS: Wheat produces a one-seeded fruit called a kernel, often called wheat berries, that is extremely high in the protein gluten. It's the simplest form of wheat and is one of the oldest cultivated grains, first grown in western Asia 6,000 years ago. It was the grain of choice during the Roman Empire.

MILLET: Millet does not contain gluten and is ranked as the least allergenic of grains. It's also extremely high in B-complex vitamins. In general, its protein content is similar to that of wheat, but it lacks the amino acid lysine so its protein content is enhanced when it is eaten with beans or other legumes.

COUSCOUS: Couscous is a favorite for camp meals. It's a grainlike pasta made by mixing flour and water to create a paste that is formed into small grains and then dried. The couscous you find at the bulk food store is most likely made from 100 percent durum wheat, but rice or corn can be used as well. It is a great side dish to accompany meats, cooks very quickly and it is excellent in salads.

QUINOA: Pronounced *keen-wa*, this grain is found in the Andean Mountains of South America. It contains all nine amino acids making it a complete protein as it has the essential one, lysine, which is missing in other grains. It also has more iron than other grains and is high in minerals and vitamins. It was a staple for the ancient Inca civilization as well as the present-day hungry camper. It takes no time to cook (even shorter than couscous) and will turn from white to transparent when done.

After the bulk food store, the next part of food preparation is to check out the local supermarket. You will be surprised at what you can pick up cheaply at the grocery store that is relatively lightweight, nutritious and nonperishable. You may have to go to the smaller specialty stores for a few hard-to-find items, but you can pick up just about everything you need at the large supermarkets. Here are a few things that can be easily found at most small and large-chain supermarkets: mini packets of mayonnaise; dried salami and beef jerky; packets of hot cereal; prepackaged rice or curry meals; prepackaged macaroni and cheese; prepackaged pasta and sauce meals; instant mashed potatoes; dried soup mixes; precooked bacon; canned or foil-packaged tuna, salmon and chicken; smoked salmon; prepackaged chili; flatbread; pita bread; English muffins; and cheese.

Packing

How you pack your food is determined by what mode of travel you choose. If you're hanging around a campground, life is basically carefree. Storage containers and a good cooler are all you really need. If you're heading into the interior, it's a little more complicated.

Every camper goes through various stages when it comes to packing. Usually they begin by taking almost everything imaginable. Then, after a few years of pain and frustration, they give up packing anything beyond the essentials. Problem is, they actually become extreme, shaving off minimal weight by doing silly things like spending a fortune on a titanium spork (a blend of a fork and spoon) or refusing to cook dessert. Eventually, most campers reach a happy medium.

Weight-watching Tips

Here are a few tips on how to find some kind of balance between minimalism and comfort:

Bulk Is Your Real Enemy

The majority of the bulk usually comes from three essential items: tent, sleeping bag and clothes. When it comes to tents your choice is simple. Aim for the smallest and lightest you can afford and spend more quality time huddled under a rain tarp during foul weather.

Go for down-filled rather than synthetic material when shopping for sleeping bags. The down bag is unmatched when it comes to warmth, weight and its ability to be compressed to the size of a miniature football. Just make sure it's packed in a watertight stuff sack.

The amount and type of clothes to bring is a little more complex. Your choice of garments is totally dependent on the season. You can't help but bring an extra fleece, long johns and wool toque during spring and fall outings. Remember to choose clothing with the highest possible performance-to-weight ratio. In warmer summer conditions, however, you only need to pack one

extra set of clothes. That's all you'll really need. Just hope for a hot, sunny day halfway through your trip so you can do laundry. How does this relate to food? Simply put, the more bulk you get rid of from your pack, the more wine or other indulgences you can bring along.

Lightweight Cookware

The weight of cookware can also add up, especially for a large group. Items such as a camp stove, fuel and cooking pots are indispensable. There are ways to limit the weight, however. First, spend the extra money and purchase the lightest stove possible and make good use of a windscreen to reduce your fuel consumption.

Second, a cheap stainless steel pot set bought at a discount store is far better than one of those new-aged titanium sets. Use a handy Swiss Army knife and a plastic fork and spoon rather than a metal one. Metal plates and bowls can also be replaced by a Frisbee. It can be used as both a plate and a bowl, and it can even be tossed around for entertainment after dinner. Scrub pads can also be left at home. A handful of pine noodles and sand works just as well and is far more sanitary.

Food Packs on the Pounds

Food can really add weight, but if you keep to homemade dehydrated food for at least 80 percent of your meals you can reduce the weight of your food pack without losing any flavor. As strange as it may sound, don't pack your food when you're hungry, as you'll have a tendency to pack too much, and keep portions, like rice or noodles, to exact measurements.

Weight in Time

The best advice is to place every item in your pack then weigh the pack on a good-quality scale. Then take everything back out and consider which items could be left at home or replaced by something lighter. Take special note of all those little extras you decide to pack along. When added together all those gadgets and gizmos can really add on the pounds. Each item should have two or more jobs. Also, limit the amount of things like ketchup, mustard and sugar. You'll never go through it all on one trip. Stash smaller amounts in containers or shop for those convenient trial packs.

Keeping Things Cool

If you're campground camping or the portages on your interior canoe trip happen to be short, or better yet nonexistent, then you definitely have the privilege of taking along a few luxury food items. After all, some dehydrated meals taste a little like munching on a cardboard box. There's nothing better than being able to have fresh meat and vegetables, at least for the first few days of your trip.

You may have the best cooler on the market, but it's still going to be difficult to keep some foods from spoiling. If you're packing into the interior for a lengthy trip then it's even more troublesome. Day three is the magic time when some food items are impossible to keep from spoiling without refrigeration. After that meat, even marinated and prefrozen, and eggs won't last.

You should plan on eating any skinned vegetables (lettuce, tomatoes) first. Veggies like cucumber and peppers can go a bit beyond the three-day period. Root vegetables (potatoes, carrots, onions, cabbages) will last the entire trip. Bread is also something that spoils quicker than you would think. Pumpernickel and rye bread will last a lot longer than sliced bread or bagels. Pita bread or tortillas are in between. After day five, though, you're going to have to start baking your own. Dairy products are also an issue. Without refrigeration, yogurt needs to be used up on day one. But see our chapter on dehydrating (pages 59–66). It will last a bit longer in colder temperatures and will last a few days in a cooler with ice. Milk and cream can only be kept in a cooler. For interior camping, why not substitute Irish cream liqueur for cream in your morning coffee?

Here are a few tips on keeping the fresh food fresh and the frozen food frozen:

- Bacon and sausages will last longer than other meats due to the high amount of preservatives they contain.

- Vacuum-sealing meats and vegetables will greatly increase their pack life. Don't go out and buy a vacuum machine right away though, as many stores will seal your purchase free of charge.

- Meat can be kept bacteria-free for up to four days by wrapping it in a piece of cheesecloth or other thin cloth that has been soaked (not saturated) in vinegar. The vinegar smell and taste disappears as soon as the meat is placed over the fire.

- To keep frozen meat from thawing out too quickly, make sure to marinate it before putting it into the freezer (the frozen marinade will act as an ice pack), store it in a freezer bag and then wrap it in newsprint or other insulating material.

- Frozen meat should be placed in the center of the food bag and kept away from direct sunlight or stored in a small cooler. Soft-sided cooler bags don't usually keep things as cool as plastic coolers, but the empty bag can easily be stuffed into your backpack.

- The crushed ice you see under the fish and seafood at the grocery store is the best ice to pack in your cooler. It lasts longer than regular ice, and the store will often give it away for free.

- Dry ice will keep items completely frozen for up to six days. As it melts, it turns directly into carbon dioxide rather than a liquid, creating no problems with freezer burn or wet food bags. It works well for meat, margarine (lasts longer than butter), ice cubes and even ice cream. But it has a tendency to burst open pop or beer cans, weighs a fair bit and can be difficult to find.

- When making salads, choose red cabbage or Chinese (also called napa) cabbage rather than a regular head of lettuce. Cabbage will keep for weeks without refrigeration and makes a tasty side dish when mixed with shredded carrots, red onion slices, red and green peppers, raisins and cashews.

- Vegetables such as tomatoes, peppers and celery will last much longer if you float them in a sink containing cold water and 2 tablespoons (30 mL) of chlorine bleach. Allow the vegetables to soak for a few minutes, air-dry them and then pack them away. The bleach will kill any surface bacteria that promote spoilage.

- The best way to chill your wine for the evening meal is to store it in a collapsible water bottle, like a Platypus, and, if you have a canoe, troll it behind you on a long rope for about a half hour or submerge it in the lake or river when you reach your campsite.

- Never break eggs from the shell and then store them in a container. Some believe this method is a way to avoid breaking eggs in storage. Little do they know, however, that once the egg leaves the shell, it instantly becomes a breeding ground for bacteria and is one sure way to get massive food poisoning on your trip. The best place to store eggs is in a Styrofoam carton, stuffed in the center of your pack or duct taped firmly under the canoe seat. You can also use liquid eggs and freeze them to last longer.

- Cheese can stay fresh much longer than you think. Purchase hard cheeses (Cheddar, mozzarella, Parmesan) and wrap them up in a vinegar-soaked cloth, or even go an extra step and dip in paraffin wax. Larger chunks store better than smaller ones.

Containers

A huge assortment of reusable containers can be used to store spices and food staples. Various sizes of wide-mouth polyethylene

bottles are great. So are plastic vitamin bottles. But make sure to double pack everything in a zipper storage bag, just in case. Also, stay away from anything that is not regulated for food storage.

There's nothing worse than looking through the entire contents of the food container before finding what you're looking for. To help eliminate the stress, try to organize everything in separate color-coded bags. For example: breakfast is blue, lunch is yellow and dinner is red. That way you'll at least know which bag to start with prior to searching for the elusive peanut butter. You can easily make your own storage containers, but have a look at Ostrom's Barrel Bags. The company has even perfected a rounded (and crushable) cooler bag that fits perfectly into a barrel.

Here are some items that should be packed separate, similar to your spice kit, and stored in zipper storage bags or containers:

- coffee (decaffeinated for those who can't have caffeine);

- tea (including herbal tea);

- hot chocolate;

- dried soup mix;

- oil;

- maple syrup;

- peanut butter;

- jam or jelly;

- honey;

- soy sauce;

- juice crystals;

- brown sugar;

- milk powder;

- margarine or butter

The Perfect Camp

A camp is a little bit of heaven. Just like at home, the kitchen has the essential items and a good number of fancy gadgets that aren't truly necessary.

Stainless-steel pots and pans (or cast iron if you don't have to carry them far) are the way to go. Aluminum is lighter and cheaper but doesn't do as good a job. A 3 quart (3 L) pot with a 2 quart (2 L) pot nestled inside is sufficient for two to four people. More than that and you'd better go with an 8 quart (8 L) pot with a 4 or 6 quart (4 or 6 L) one nestled inside.

Some campers think it's an absolute sin to use pots over a campfire rather than a camp stove due to them getting blackened by the soot from the fire. Others believe the charcoaled color adds character and even adds flavor to the food. If you follow the second philosophy then just make sure to store the pot set in a separate storage bag and pack a pair of cooking gloves. Coating the outside of the pot with soap also helps minimize the amount of soot collected.

Extreme lightweight campers use a pot lid as a frying pan. It's the handle of the frying pan that makes it difficult to pack, so either remove the handle from the pan after you buy it or simply buy one without a handle — just make sure to take a pot-gripper. A griddle can also be used when cooking for larger groups, perfect for a couple rows of flapjacks surrounded by bacon. Combine the griddle with a firebox or campfire grill and you can make some amazing meals for large groups.

Apart from everyone having a knife, fork and spoon (or spork), extra utensils that come in handy include a whisk, cheese grater,

large spoon and a spatula. Buy mini versions of these utensils when you see them at stores or garage sales.

Campers usually prefer reusable plastic plates. However, there are all sorts of specialized lightweight choices out there. Drinking mugs can be enamel or stainless steel, but an insulated mug is far more handy. A good rule to follow is to make sure that your mugs will fit snugly inside your pot set. Today there is a huge assortment of reusable containers available that can be used to store spices and foods. Various sizes of wide-mouth polyethylene bottles are great. So are plastic vitamin bottles. But make sure to double pack everything in zipper storage bags, just in case.

Food Handling

We all know you should wash your hands before handling food. However, some people don't do it while camping because they find it a hassle. Some campers have the strange notion that being unhygienic is a part of the real camping experience. Not true. One of the most common ways for sickness to plague a group, and ruin

a trip, is for someone to handle the food without washing up first.

The trick to safe food handling is to make it hassle-free to wash up (or to guilt everyone into making sure they wash up). The best overall method for hassle-free washing is to have two cleaning kits: one stored with the kitchen gear and the other in the toiletry bag.

The kit in the kitchen gear is a no-brainer. The cook will see the hand soap and/or alcohol hand sanitizer among the pots and pans and most likely make use of it before preparing a meal. If they don't, other campers will surely notice and most likely make a comment. It's the toiletry bag that's the problem. Individual campers can say they've washed up, or even pretend to do so, but who's to say they actually did (yes, this happens more than you'd want to know). So the trick is to hang a communal toiletry bag in a tree or somewhere just as obvious the moment you set up camp. It should consist of the usual items, such as toilet paper, wet wipes, bug repellent, a flashlight and maybe some light reading material. Then attach a second bag with hand soap and/or alcohol hand sanitizer. The entire kit should also have a big red bandana or bright yellow ribbon tied to it. Give instructions to the group that when someone has to use the facilities (whether it's an outhouse at the campground or a latrine in the interior), the toiletry bag(s) goes with them. This works twofold: it will allow some privacy to anyone who's using the facilities — basically if the toiletry kit is gone then no one else is allowed to wander off to accidentally witness someone pooping in the woods — and it applies a bit of indirect peer pressure from members of the group to make sure everyone uses the soap or hand sanitizer.

Dish Washing

The most effective way to wash dishes is to fill a large cooking pot or lightweight collapsible basin with warm, soapy water (use biodegradable soap). Never do dishes directly in a lake or river. For a scrub brush use a handful of pine needles, sand or leaves off the forest floor. It sounds crazy, but pine needles do a better

job than wet sponges or scrub pads, which are breeding grounds for bacteria.

Once the dishes are done, take the gray water well away from the campsite and dispose of it in a small hole created by kicking up the first layer of topsoil with the heel of your boot. It will become part of the soil in a couple of weeks. Never get rid of the gray water in a lake or river. Biodegradable soap only biodegrades in soil, where bacteria and enzymes exist to begin the process. Food scraps or leftovers can be burned in a hot campfire or packed out in a separate sealable plastic bag or container.

One last process to do to make sure no one gets sick from bacteria on the trip is to place the dishes on top of a small ground tarp and pour boiled water over them. Then, let the dishes air dry rather then use the same drying towel over and over, which is also a breeding ground for bacteria.

Critter Proofing

Keeping your food safe from bears (and other critters) is an important element of any camping trip. Not only do you want to reduce the chances of having an unwanted close encounter with a bear, raccoon or field mouse, you also don't want to lose your food.

There are a number of ways to store your food. If you're at a campground you can make use of your vehicle — just make darn sure the food is also packed in sealable containers. A bear, or even a raccoon, can smell a meal a mile away and can make a real mess when trying to break into your car. Also, never store food or anything else with a sweet odor (toothpaste, hand lotion, deodorant) in your tent.

Handling a Bear Encounter

This is the most-asked question. It's also the most difficult one to answer. In a perfect scenario this is what you should do:

First, never run. Running away may trigger a prey-predator response, and a bear can outrun the best Olympic athlete. You could climb a tree, but black bears and young grizzlies can climb trees better than you can. It's best to stay put and assess the situation. If you stay put the bear may eventually move on, and the encounter becomes an enjoyable experience.

But what if it charges you instead? Well, in most circumstances the bear is faking it. But you wouldn't know the difference between a real charge and a pretend one, so the next move is to sex it before you make your move. If it's a male bear (more so a black bear), then a mild aggression technique may work (making lots of noise and standing erect, waving your arms in the air). It's rare, but male bears have been known to stalk and hunt humans for food, and the only way to protect yourself against a predacious bear is to fight back. Really fight back. However, if you try to be aggressive with a female, especially one with cubs, then she is most likely to attack in defense. You're best to play dead. Lie face down with your hands wrapped around your neck to protect your vital organs and spread your legs somewhat apart to help anchor yourself in case the bear attempts to flip you over. This maneuver is also said to be the best defense against grizzly bears.

There are items that have proven effective in protecting yourself against bear attacks. Bear bangers and pepper spray are the most commonly used. The bangers are considered the less harmful and safest deterrent, but they're obviously not as effective as pepper spray if the bear attacks. You'll probably never use the can of bear spray, but having it packed along gives you some sense of security. However, it can also make a bad situation worse. A number of campers have blasted at a bear and had the spray blow right back into their face. There's also the story about the tripper in Jasper National Park who sprayed his tent with the pepper, thinking it would keep bears away. That night a grizzly wandered into the man's camp and, actually finding the spray tasty, ate his tent and accidentally injured the occupant in the process.

Hanging Food in a Tree

The most notable method of storing food safely is hanging. First, load all food, and anything else with strong odors (toothpaste, sunscreen, hand lotion, soap, scented bug repellent) in a separate pack, barrel pack or waterproof bag. Then, string it up over an

outstretched limb or between two trees. Whichever you choose, make sure to set up the bear rope early in the evening so you just have to go and pull the food pack up before bed. There's nothing worse than looking for a proper tree to hang your food in when it's pitch dark. Also, make sure to choose a tree well away from camp, at least 90 feet (30 m) into the forest and away from well-used trails. A bear, especially in a well-used park, will quickly get to know each campsite's food cache if it's easy to locate.

It helps to tie a piece of fluorescent flagging tape onto the bear rope. It's not all that easy to relocate a rope hanging in the back bush when it's time to rig the food bag up, and the flagging tape helps more than you can imagine.

Pulley System

For the first few days of a trip, the food bag may be a little too heavy to lift. Try bringing two sections of rope, one with a small metal pulley (found at any hardware store) tied to one end. Throw the pulley rope over the branch and pass the other rope through the pulley. Then tie the other end of the pulley rope to a tree and hoist up the heavy pack with the other rope. The pulley also adds a good weight on the end of the rope while tossing the rope over a single limb or over the rope tied between two trees.

Food Barrels

Some canoeists have opted to use barrels for keeping their food safe. They're a great system to keep everything dry and relatively odor-free, and they can come in handy when traveling in the far North, where there are no tall trees to hang your food from. But in

no way should they be considered "bear barrels." In the last few years there have been numerous reports about campers who have placed their food barrel right beside their tent being woken up by a bear smashing it to pieces. Algonquin Park in Ontario, Canada, has even reported that in the last few years bears have gotten to know that a blue barrel means food, just as Yogi identified a picnic basket, and have ripped open a number of barrels to get the contents. Remember, if a bear can break into a car with one swing of a paw, then a thin plastic barrel is no match for it. There are, however, food storage barrels available from some outdoor stores specifically designed to be "bear proof." They're ideal for kayaking or rafting but too awkward to pack for backpacking or canoeing.

Safe Drinking Water

If you think being in a remote wilderness area means the water you find is safe to drink, think again! There are so many pollutants and pathogens floating around in our lakes and streams that the days of dipping your cup directly into the water for a drink are long gone.

Water contaminants

One of the worst bugs to pick up is *Giardia lamblia*. The tiny cyst gets into the water cycle by being deposited with the feces of an infected animal. The usual host is the beaver, which is how this waterborne pathogen got its nickname, "beaver fever," but it can be deposited by any mammal, including humans.

It only takes 10 giardia cysts to infect your body. The microscopic protozoan, measuring 21 microns in length (the tip of a sewing needle measures 700 microns), hatches inside the small intestine, incubates for a period from five days to several months, reproduces like wildfire, establishes a colony and then has a little party in your gut, making you feel as if Montezuma has moved north to seek his revenge.

Symptoms can be severe or completely unnoticeable. They include diarrhea, abdominal cramps, fatigue, weight loss, flatulence and nausea — not a pleasant experience while being away from flush toilets and a local pharmacy. Usually, however, you only experience symptoms once home and then just assume it's the flu. However, if the cyst does not get treated, it can cause severe problems. I've been affected three times, and each case took over a month to treat with antibiotics.

Giardia is the most common pathogen to find swimming around in your water bottle. The good news, however, is that it's the least dangerous. Tularemia is a little more serious. It is a plaguelike disease that infects humans and more than 80 percent of other species of mammal. It is caused by a bacterium, which multiplies rapidly through the bloodstream, invading cells of the liver, spleen, lungs, kidneys and lymph nodes.

When a person is infected by tularemia they can expect the worst flulike symptoms: a high temperature, headaches, chills, sweating, nausea, vomiting and body pain. Extreme symptoms, as if the others aren't bad enough, are a swollen area where the infection entered (hand, arm, face or neck), inflammation of the eye membrane and general enlargement of the lymph nodes.

This parasitic protozoan can be transmitted the same way as giardia — ingestion of water contaminated by either the feces or the carcass of an infected mammal. It can also be given by inoculation from biting insects (bloodsucking flies, ticks, lice or fleas). A very high number of trappers catch this disease due to their constant contact with the internal organs and body fluids of mammals.

In addition to giardia and tularemia, there are many varieties of bacteria floating around in the water supply as well. E. coli gives you a nasty case of the trots, *Klebsiella pneumoniae* causes pneumonia and salmonella can give you either a bad case of food poisoning or a bout of typhoid fever. Then there are surface-water pollutants like gas fuel, pesticides and heavy metals from old mine sites. All of these are very good reasons to treat all water while you're out there.

Water Treatments

Boiling

Boiling is probably the most common method to kill germs. Boiling water for five minutes will eliminate most of everything, and just having it come to a rolling boil is sufficient enough to get rid of protozoa, bacteria and even viruses. The problem with boiling all the water you'll need, however, is that it's quite simply a waste of stove fuel. What usually happens is that the water boiled the night before quickly runs out halfway through the day. So rather than stopping to boil up some more, which would be rather silly on a hot day, campers either don't drink at all, making them severely dehydrated, or get lazy and just drink water directly from the lake.

Chemical Treatment

Iodine tablets are another option for cleaning water. The chemical kills most of what's out there. It should be noted, however, that there's a strong odor, not to mention a bland taste, to the water. And there's also a warning, "use only for emergencies," placed in fine print on the bottom of the label.

The other dilemma with using iodine is that it kills both the bad bacteria in the water and the good bacteria that are in your stomach and help you digest. After frequent use this can cause a problem.

For infrequent use, however, using iodine is easy and effective. The dose is one tablet for every quart (or liter) of water and then waiting 15 minutes, or use two tablets if the water is cloudy or colder than 50°F (10°C) and wait for one hour. To get rid of the bad taste of the treated water, simply disguise it by adding flavor crystals, such as Tang.

You can purify water by passing it through fine mesh filters containing iodine. The iodine is only released when there are microorganisms present. The temperature of the water is irrelevant, and your water doesn't get "spiked" with iodine unless it needs it. The disadvantage is the need to figure out when to change the iodine-laced filters.

There are other chemicals that are just as effective. Some campers trust in adding a few drops of bleach to their water bottle. Others have changed over to a new system called Aquamira. This chemical treatment, produced by McNett Company, directly kills the bacteria and works by releasing oxygen in a highly controlled form. It has no bad taste or odor and two 1-ounce (30 mL) containers can purify 30 gallons (114 L) of water.

Filters

The best purification system for drinking water is a filter. You just pump and drink. And by making water collection so quick and easy, there's less chance of becoming dehydrated.

There are a few disadvantages, starting with the high cost. The main body of the system itself is not that bad, but the price of the replacement filters is outrageous. If you only go on a one-week trip per year then the filter should last you a couple of years. But if you're out all season you're going to use up at least one or two filters, which cost close to $40 each. The only way to save money is to always wash the filter out after each trip. It's also a great idea to wrap a coffee filter around it to help extend the use.

Filters strain out microscopic contaminants like giardia, but they don't necessarily eliminate bacteria or viruses. The purity of the water greatly relies on the size of the filter's pores. A pore size of two microns or smaller will get rid of nasty pathogens like giardia and surface pollutants. However, it takes a pore size of less than 0.4 microns to remove bacteria and viruses.

Campfires

What is it about campfires? Why are they so vivid in our memories of camping out? The flickering light, sparks spiraling into the night sky, the warmth radiating from the inner circle. To say that a campfire appeals to us because it gives us warmth and light would be correct, but that's not the complete reason. It may be that it connects all of us to our primitive ancestors who depended dearly on the heat campfires generated for pure survival. But circling a fire ring with green sticks poked through puffy marshmallows can't relate back to our primordial instincts. Again, it has to be much more than that.

Campfires give us a lot of pleasures, but the very idea of sitting around a campfire, whether it's in a group or alone, is what signifies that you've finally begun to slow down. Your senses open up. A campfire starts to sound good, look good and smell good. You can distinctly hear the snap of exploding resin, watch as the flames change color as the fire absorbs oxygen, and smell the smoke being emitted from logs of maple, birch or pine. Put simply, lighting a campfire signifies that your time spent in the wilderness has begun.

Safe Ax Handling

To safely split wood with a camp ax, begin by sawing sections of a log. Anything smaller in diameter than your forearm you can simply throw in the fire, but any bigger pieces should be split with the ax. Set the piece of wood upright, place the blade of the ax across the center of the log and then strike the top of the ax head with another piece of wood. The ax works as an effective splitting edge rather than a cutting tool. No swinging is involved, which greatly decreases the chance of injury — and ruining a perfectly good camping vacation.

How to Light a One-Match Fire

Starting the evening fire with just one match is the biggest challenge to a group of campers. It beats catching the biggest fish or carrying the heaviest load, and the stakes get higher the more foul the weather.

First, go far back behind camp to collect a handful of dead and dry pencil-sized twigs. Drier twigs will be under the forest canopy. Next, locate a downed tree and, with one of those collapsible camp saws, saw off the end not touching the ground (wood touching the ground will quickly rot) into pieces no greater than the length and thickness of an arm. To check if it's dry throughout, simply touch the cut end with your tongue. You'll be able to taste the dampness in the wood.

Use thin strips of birch bark, dry pine needles, a glob of pitch squeezed from balsam blisters or a piece of dried lichen as a fire starter, or use a homemade fire starter (see below) and place it at the base of the fire ring.

Place the pencil-sized twigs in a crisscross pattern over the fire-starter material. Next, place the larger pieces on top, but make sure there's plenty of space for the fire to breathe (too much smoke means you're smothering the flames). Place a few more pencil-sized twigs on top to lock everything in place.

Ignite the fire-starter material with a match stored in a waterproof container (to make sure the match is dry, place a cotton ball on top of the matches in the container and briskly run the match through your hair before igniting it to draw out any moisture).

Construct a second pile of wood around and even on top of the fire to constantly dry out your fuel source.

Homemade Fire Starters

- A cotton ball dipped in petroleum jelly and stored in a waterproof container

- A strip of inner tube

- A ball of steel wool

- Strips of waxed paper

Smoke Charmer

Ever heard the phrase "I hate white rabbits" being yelled out around the fire ring to chase the smoke away? The phrase seems more than a little odd, but the darn expression seems to work. The smoke will mysteriously drift over to the next person in your group. But does the superstition have any merit? Well, not really. It seems the whole thing originated from the idea that white rabbits were considered an omen of death and that, in England, good luck would come upon you if you called out "white rabbit" three times on the first of every month. The poor white bunnies have been cursed ever since.

- Pieces of wax crayon

- Birthday candles or tea lights

- Sawdust or dryer lint dipped in melted paraffin and stored in an egg carton

- A few strips of duct tape rolled up in a ball and coated with a few squirts of bug repellent (this is my favorite)

- Squirt of alcohol-based hand sanitizer

- Lip balm

- Potato chips or, better still, tortilla chips

Campfire Cooking Tips

- Small fires are easier and better to cook on.

- Avoid direct flame since it will burn the outside of food but keep the inside uncooked.

- Wait until the wood has burned down to embers.

- Increase the cooking heat by piling the coals closer together and reduce it by spreading them apart.

- A blanket of ash covering the coals acts as an insulator and controls the heat better for cooking, especially for potatoes, corn or onions wrapped in foil.

- To reduce smoke try burning dried wood from a beaver lodge; it's sun dried with no resin or outer bark, reducing smoke in a big way.

- Softwood like pine and spruce may be good to get the fire started, but hardwood like maple or oak provides a far better heat for cooking.

- Using a camp grill is far better than trying to balance pots on a stick hanging over the fire.

- Build a windbreak with rocks.

- Use the edge of the fire to keep items already cooked warm while you prepare the rest of the meal.

Fireboxes

Campfires are not as efficient when it comes to cooking meals, but there's still some sense of the mystic to them. To improve the campfire's cooking abilities, use a grill or firebox.

The Environmental Fireplace, or firebox, was an idea of canoeist and filmmaker Bill Mason, who then had Ric Driediger at Horizons Unlimited mass-produce it for environmentally conscious campers. The basic idea is to contain the campfire rather than build a traditional campfire ring, which would inevitably leave a blackened mark on the forest floor. It also consumes only half the wood to cook up dinner or boil a pot of water for coffee or tea.

Using a campfire with a simple grill balanced overtop takes a bit of skill. The rocks circling the fire have to be placed and then replaced to make sure the cooking pot sits flat over the flames. Fireboxes give you far more control over your cooking flames. There are lots of designs out there — even homemade versions made from a large tin can and metal cutters — but they're generally a metal box with a grilled top. They're also foldable, so they can be placed in a storage bag.

What makes a firebox more efficient is that it uses less wood than a regular campfire and concentrates the heat into a more confined and controlled area.

Camp Stoves

Cooking on a campfire may be traditional to some, but it's not that easy. First you have to light it, and then there's no easy way to control the flames. It's usually too hot and you end up burning everything or it's died down to embers and you're waiting forever for the water to boil.

That's why a camp stove is a better choice for cooking a good camp meal. However, realizing the benefits of cooking on a camp stove rather than a campfire is much simpler than figuring out which stove to buy. Here's a general breakdown to help you decide which one to purchase, based mainly on fuel types, cost and how much heat it produces.

Butane

Many campers find butane models ideal. It is a clean-burning, reliable and trouble-free stove that operates on a pressurized canister (of butane) that is attached to the stove. The flame can be controlled easily and placed at a simmer, unlike many of the other stove models. It also sells at a good price. The only disadvantage, apart from butane not working well in cold temperatures, is that you have to carry the empty canisters out with you and drop them off at a designated recycling center (finding replacement canisters at outdoor stores can also be an issue).

RIGHT Primus classic butane trail stove

Propane

Propane outperforms butane in cold temperatures. It also produces one of the cleanest flames, which is also incredibly easy to adjust. Propane stove owners still have to deal with the empty canister dilemma. However, they make a good, inexpensive stove, especially for campground camping.

White Gas

White gas is an excellent choice. The stove models are more expensive than most other fuel-type designs; however, since white gas is relatively cheap to buy, and there are no separate cylinders to purchase, they are actually less expensive in the long run. White-gas stoves also require priming, which can be a real hassle, but they are also far more efficient in cold temperatures.

ABOVE LEFT   Optimus Climber white gas stove

ABOVE RIGHT   MSR Whisperlite white gas stove

RIGHT   The Outback Oven with a MSR Dragonfly white gas stove

Alcohol Stove

Campers in Canada and the United States are fixated on petroleum-based stoves, but everywhere else in the world it's alcohol stoves that rule; especially the Trangia, made in Sweden. The stove itself has many advantages. First, it's extremely lightweight. It also comes with its own cook set and is quite compact. They're also very simple, meaning there's nothing much to them and nothing much can go wrong with them. The Trangia resembles a fancy fondue set. Most importantly, they're unbelievably quiet.

There are some disadvantages though. Depending on what fuel you use, it's difficult to see the flame when it's on. It also has a longer boiling time than all pressurized petroleum-based stoves. The most common fuel is methyl hydrate — also known as methanol, wood alcohol or wood spirits. This clean-burning fuel is

The Trangia Stove can run on various types of alcohol, including brake-line anti-freeze, methanol-hydrate (wood alcohol) or even fondue fuel.

widely available at hardware and paint stores and provides the best power density of all the fuels we tested. It is, however, poisonous (don't drink it or spill it into waterways) and can be absorbed through the skin, so care should be taken when handling it.

How Much Fuel Do I Bring Along?

The amount of fuel needed has so many variables: fuel type, the air temperature, the wind and the design of windscreen used, the maximum heat output (BTU) of the stove, even the type of pots and pans used. Overall, however, the best way to judge your fuel consumption is to plan 40 minutes of cooking time for dinner and 20 minutes for preparing a hot breakfast. Let's say you're going on a five-day trip. That adds up to four dinners (2 hours and 40 minutes of burning time) and four breakfasts (1 hour and 20 minutes). Now add an extra hour for a couple of hot soups for lunch or an unexpected cold-weather snap that will rob you of extra fuel. So, to be on the safe side, you can say you need a little more than 5 hours of fuel for a five-day trip. If your stove runs on white gas and burns quickly and hot like the MSR models, with a pump/fuel bottle, it will use up a 34-fluid ounce (1 L) bottle of fuel every three days, which means you need to bring 60 fluid ounces (2 L) for five days to be on the safe side. Alcohol-based stoves generally burn a little more than white-gas stoves. If you have a butane or propane stove, which run on pressurized canisters, then two canisters should be enough, with a little to spare. Also, pack a windscreen and/or a pot cozy to save fuel, and keep the lid on the pot — no peeking.

In conclusion, if you're a speed demon out on a camping or tripping expedition and need hot water NOW, the pressurized gas stove is the stove for you. The heat from the alcohol stove, on the other hand, in addition to being completely silent, makes for great cooking — no instant scorch like with pressurized gas, just nice, steady, even heat — perfect for sautéing veggies or making fry bread.

Stick Stoves

A more environmentally friendly stove design is one that uses sticks, pinecones and other small forest debris (even animal dung) rather than a petroleum product or alcohol. There are a number of them on the market. The Kelly Kettle, however, is one of the best overall stick stoves on the market.

What sets the Kelly Kettle apart from all other stick stoves is the ingenious double-wall chimney design.

My introduction to the Kelly Kettle was during a family canoe trip in northern Scotland. I knew nothing about it and was somewhat skeptical about using it. By the end of the trip, however, I was captivated by the kettle and have used it on countless other trips since.

It's basically a stick stove, requiring no petroleum- or alcohol-based fuel. But what sets it apart from all other stick stoves is the ingenious double-wall chimney design. You simply light sticks, small bits of wood, pinecones and other combustible material in the base plate. The flames are then drawn upward through a fire chamber, which acts like a chimney draft. The water is stored in a water jacket around the chimney, which rapidly boils the water, even in the worst wet and windy weather conditions.

The main disadvantage of the Kelly Kettle is that it's bulky. An aluminum design can replace the regular stainless steel to lighten it up. A cooking accessory can also be placed on top of

the chimney spout to hold a small pot or frying pan. Just make sure to keep water in the chamber or you'll melt the kettle.

There's countless recipes that can be cooked up in a classic cast iron Dutch Oven.

Dutch Oven

The Dutch oven originated in Holland around the early 1700s and has been widely used around the world ever since. It's heavy and bulky but whatever is cooked in it tastes fantastic — and it cooks just about anything. Simply place above a fire (see image). Dutch ovens are commonly made from cast iron. The material distributes heat evenly and retains heat, which is why the oven is so effective. The solid lid seals the pot and steams the contents, keeping in the moisture so the food is tender. Cast iron is also long lasting, and these pots can literally be passed down from generation to generation.

Ovens — Baking in the Bush

In his 1943 book *The Incomplete Anglers*, author John D. Robins heavily criticizes his paddling partner during a trip across Ontario's Algonquin Park for toasting the bread before its time. Traditionally, it was forbidden to toast bread until a week or so into a trip, simply because that gave it the longest shelf life. After a week the bread would be going stale and moldy, and toasting it was a good way to get a few more days out of it.

The question is, why didn't they bake their own while on the trip? There's really no excuse not to bake fresh bread, or anything else for that matter, while camping out. Reflector ovens were definitely around during Robins' trip and are still used today; Dutch ovens have become commonplace in many outdoor kitchen sets; and a product called the Outback Oven has revolutionized the process of baking up brownies, cakes and pies.

Outback Ovens are a lightweight baking system that can be used with pressurized-gas camp stoves. The main component is the heat-diffuser at the base, which allows the heat to be evenly distributed. A hood — resembling a tea cozy — is then placed over the Teflon-coated pan. Just make sure to use a stove model that can simmer or at least puts out an even heat. You'll have a lot of burned food if not. Also, make sure that the gas cylinder is separate and away from the burner. If not, the hood, when placed over the pot and stove, will heat up the pressurized gas cylinder and may cause it to explode.

Making use of a reflector oven can dramatically alter a trip. It's not a necessary piece of kitchen gear by any means, but once you try it out you'll never go on a camping trip without one. The benefits definitely override the weight and bulk. Imagine fresh bread, pita pizza, blueberry pie, brownies, muffins — all on day 10 of a 20-day trip. They're made of either lightweight aluminum or stainless steel and concave in design. Placing the oven beside the campfire reflects the radiant heat inside and evenly bakes whatever is sitting on the wire rack. The angle has to be watched now and then to moderate the amount of heat, and it's best to wait so there's a good bed of coals before you start baking. The better models fold down to fit inside a pack.

Double Boiler

You don't need any of the fancier gadgets to bake, as long as you packed two pots and a plastic bag. Here's how to bake bread:

- In a heavy-duty zipper freezer bag, mix 2 cups (500 mL) flour, 1 teaspoon (5 mL) sugar, 1 package yeast, 6 tablespoons (90 mL) powdered milk, 1 teaspoon (5 mL) oil and ½ cup (125 mL) hot water.
- Squeeze the upper part of the bag to force out the air and then shake and work the bag with your fingers to blend the ingredients.
- Remove the mixture from the bag and knead it on a floured surface.
- Place the formed bread back into the bag and let it rise for 10 minutes.
- Fill the larger of the two pots with 1 inch (2.5 cm) water, and then rest the second pot on top of the water (this acts as a heat diffuser).
- Place the bagged bread in the smaller pot and loosely roll down the top of the bag (don't seal it).
- Place a lid on the larger pot and boil until the bread is baked (should take 20–30 minutes).

Dehydrating Food

When camping at a campground, you may have the luxury of a plug-in fridge or a cooler full of ice to keep fresh food from going bad. Packing for the interior is a different story! It's possible to take fresh food for the first three days, but after that you risk getting food poisoning. Fresh foods are also heavy to carry. By packing dehydrated foods, you'll not only remove the water (and reduce the weight considerably), you'll eliminate the problem of bacteria forming and making you sick. Drying your own food is by far the best way to prepare camp meals, and it's a lot less expensive (and more fun) than buying prepackaged dehydrated ones

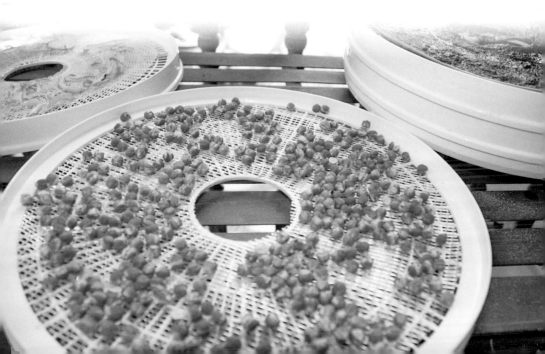

You can pick up a good food dehydrator for less than $100, but you can also place items on racks in your oven and use a cookie sheet, coated with a layer of cooking oil, to dehydrate sauces. Set the oven at the lowest temperature possible and leave for 6 to 8 hours. You can use a toothpick to keep the door open a little to help keep the air circulating, especially if you have a gas stove. This method is perfect for sauces and meats but may be too hot to properly prepare fruits and vegetables, depending on the stove.

Sauces are best to practice on. A jar of spaghetti sauce placed in the dehydrator or oven is reduced to a thin slice of what looks like fruit leather. Once at camp, simply place the dried sauce in a small amount of boiling water (about ½ cup/125 mL); it turns right back into the original spaghetti sauce.

Meat must be cooked before drying. Some meats, such as cooked ground beef, should also be rinsed over and over again with hot water to eliminate the grease content and reduce the chances of bacteria forming. Drying ground turkey or ground venison is an amazing way to add substance to a camp meal. It has less fat and therefore less chance of spoiling while you are out on the trip.

Some dried foods are best bought directly at the bulk food store. Onions and garlic really stink up the house when dried in the dehydrator, and banana chips and dried pineapple slices are difficult to make. Avoid dehydrating strong-smelling foods (e.g., mushrooms, asparagus) with other foods if you don't want everything smelling the same. Some fruits (blueberries, cherries) should be pierced with a toothpick prior to drying to drain juice and speed up the drying process. Vegetables that you generally don't eat raw should also be blanched first, boiling them in water or steaming them. This scalding action destroys naturally occurring enzymes that contribute to flavor loss, texture change and color change during storage.

Dehydrating Guidelines

The temperatures and times for each foodstuff are based on a purchased food dehydrator.

Dehydrating Fruit

Apples

Preparation: Peel and core the apple and cut crossways to form ¼-inch (0.5 cm) thick rings. Prevent browning by dipping in lemon juice prior to drying.

Time: 6–8 hours

Is it done? Apple slices should be dry but leathery and still flexible.

Apricots

Preparation: Remove pit and cut fruit lengthwise in quarters. Prevent browning by dipping in lemon juice prior to drying.

Time: 10–20 hours

Is it done? Should be dry but leathery and still flexible.

Cranberries

Preparation: Cut berries in half.

Time: 8–10 hours

Is it done? Should be dry and leathery but no longer tacky inside.

Mangoes

Preparation: Peel with vegetable peeler, cut around pit and slice fruit into ¼-inch (0.5 cm) pieces. Use ripe but not overripe mangos.

Time: 10–12 hours

Is it done? Should be dry, leathery but still flexible.

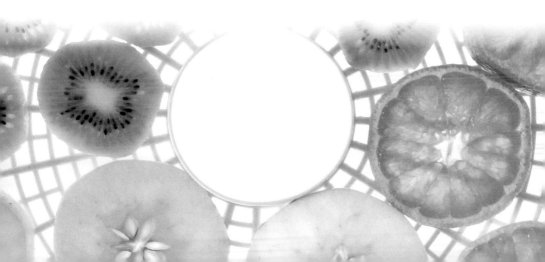

Peaches

Preparation: Pit and slice into ½-inch (1 cm) pieces (peel if desired, but not necessary). Prevent browning by dipping in lemon juice prior to drying.

Time: 10–12 hours

Is it done? Should be dry, leathery but still flexible.

Pears

Preparation: Remove core and slice fruit into ½-inch (1 cm) pieces. To prevent browning, dip in lemon juice prior to drying.

Time: 10–12 hours

Is it done? Should be dry, leathery but still flexible.

Plums

Preparation: Cut plum lengthwise into wedges (about ½ inch/1 cm thick); pierce skin multiple times with toothpick.

Time: 10–12 hours

Is it done? Should be dry, leathery and no longer juicy but still flexible.

Strawberries

Preparation: Remove stems and slice berries lengthwise into ¼-inch (0.5 cm) thick pieces. Locally grown fresh strawberries dry much better than the ones shipped to the grocery store.

Time: 8–10 hours

Is it done? Should be dry, leathery and no longer juicy but still flexible.

Dehydrating Vegetables

Asparagus

Preparation: Blanch for 3 minutes, place into cold water and then remove tough ends and cut into 1-inch (2.5 cm) lengths.

Time: 12–14 hours

Is it done? Should feel dry and crisp with no sign of moisture throughout.

Broccoli

Preparation: Break off tops into ½ inch (1 cm) sections and discard thick, woody stems. Blanch tops for 2 minutes and place into cold water

Time: 6–8 hours

Is it done? Should feel dry and crisp with no moisture throughout.

Carrots

Preparation: Peel the skin and cut carrots crosswise into ¼-inch (0.5 cm) pieces.

Time: 6–8 hours

Is it done? Dry and crisp but still a little bit flexible.

Corn

Preparation: Simply use canned corn or frozen corn. If using fresh corn, cook cobs in boiling water and cut kernels off cob.

Time: 10–12 hours

Is it done? Should have a shriveled look and be firm but brittle to touch.

Cucumber

Preparation: Use cucumbers with thinner skin and smaller seeds so there will be no need to peel or seed. Cut off ends and discard. Slice crosswise into ¼-inch (0.5 cm) pieces.

Time: 6–8 hours

Is it done? Should feel dry and crisp with no sign of moisture.

Eggplant

Preparation: Cut crosswise into ¼-inch (0.5 cm) slices. Remove the skin or leave it on. Smaller varieties of eggplant are less bitter.

Time: 8–10 hours

Is it done? Should feel firm and leathery but still flexible.

Mushrooms

Preparation: Cut lengthwise into ¼-inch (0.5 cm) pieces.

Time: 6–8 hours

Is it done? Should be dry and crisp with no sign of moisture.

Peas

Preparation: For canned or frozen peas, place on trays of a food dehydrator or a cookie sheet for the oven. For fresh peas, blanch for 2 minutes and rinse in cold water.

Time: 6–8 hours

Is it done? Should be shriveled and brittle.

Sweet Peppers

Preparation: Remove core and discard. Slice lengthwise into ¼-inch (0.5 cm) pieces.

Time: 10–12 hours

Is it done? Should feel dry and crisp with no sign of moisture.

Tomatoes

Preparation: Slice crosswise into ¼-inch to ½-inch (0.5 to 1 cm) pieces.

Time: 10–12 hours

Is it done? Should feel dry but slightly pliable and with no sign of moisture.

Zucchini

Preparation: Cut off ends; slice crosswise into ¼-inch (0.5 cm) pieces. No need to remove skin.

Time: 6–8 hours

Is it done? Should feel dry and crisp with no sign of moisture.

Dehydrating Meat & Seafood

Chicken
Preparation: Either use canned chunks of chicken or cook a chicken, remove fat and cut pieces of meat into thin strips or grind it up in a food processor.
Time: 8–15 hours
Is it done? Should be brittle and flaky with no sign of moisture.

Ground Beef
Preparation: Cook in a skillet until meat is no longer pink throughout. Then place it in a strainer and poor hot water overtop. This will rinse away any grease left over from cooking it and greatly enhance the drying process. Now transfer meat onto a paper towel to blot away the excess moisture. Season to taste. Place on a food dehydrator or a cookie sheet if using the oven.
Time: 8–12 hours
Is it done? Should be brittle with no sign of moisture.

Shrimp
Preparation: Peel and devein the shrimp. Slice in half lengthwise. Now cook shrimp in salted boiling water for 2–3 minutes (just until firm or opaque). Place in cold water, let cool and drain well. Transfer cooked shrimp onto a paper towel to blot away the

Turkey Jerky

Purchase meats with the least fat. A round roast or chicken works well. Even tofu can be done, but by far the best is turkey. Slice the meat across the grain and marinate for 2–4 hours in ½ cup (125 mL) Worcestershire sauce, ½ cup (125 mL) soy sauce and ¼ cup (60 mL) red wine vinegar. Then lay the slices across the oven racks and dry overnight (8–12 hours) at 150°F (65°C). If it snaps in half when bent, it's done. You can simply snack on it or add it to soups or stews.

excess moisture. Place them on a food dehydrator tray or a cookie sheet, if using the oven.

Time: 4–6 hours

Is it done? Should feel firm and slightly pliable.

Yogurt or Cottage Cheese

Preparation: Use 1% yogurt or 1% cottage cheese to keep it from going rancid. Don't use yogurts with gelatin or other thickeners (they won't dry all the way through). Place yogurt or cottage cheese onto sauce tray when using the dehydrator or an oiled cookie sheet for the oven. Smooth it out into consistent thickness, about ¼-inch (0.5 cm) thick. Rotate tray every couple of hours and flip over yogurt or cottage cheese halfway through the drying time.

Time: 10–14 hours

Is it done? Should peel off tray like fruit leather, or even have a brittle appearance with no sign of moisture. Dried yogurt or cottage cheese should be stored in the refrigerator and only has about a 1-week shelf life at room temperature.

Beans

Preparation: Drain and rinse either canned or cooked beans (kidney beans, black beans, white (navy) beans, Romano beans, or chickpeas will work). Place on drying tray.

Time: 5–6 hours

Is it done? Beans should be dry, crisp and light.

Breakfasts

7

Yes, breakfast is the most important meal of the day, as our mothers have always told us. It is especially true when heading out for an active outing while camping. Balance is very important in all meal choices, and since you have had a fast of possibly 8 to 10 hours, breakfast is the time to refuel your body. This chapter provides some recipes for cooked and cold breakfasts, some of which need no preparation since the work was done at home. You get the idea — we try to make breakfast very interesting while understanding it needs to be a "quick off the mark" meal.

Camp-Style Pain au Chocolate

Since you probably don't have access to a patisserie, try this version while at camp. It's an easy and delicious way to replicate Pain au Chocolate.

Serves 2

Preparation time:
5 minutes

Cooking time:
4 minutes

2	pieces pita bread, split	2
	dark chocolate squares	

Heat a nonstick skillet over medium-low heat. Insert several squares of chocolate into the open pitas (the number will vary based on pita size). Grill pitas for several minutes per side or until chocolate melts.

Cinnamon French Toast

French toast can be made at the last minute, but we think the easiest way to get a fast start in the morning is to soak the bread the night before. When coffee is brewing in the morning, you will be ready to start grilling the toast. People of all ages enjoy this recipe!

Serves 2 to 4

Preparation time:
10 minutes

Cooking time:
2 minutes per side

3	eggs	3
⅓ cup	milk	75 mL
1 tsp	ground cinnamon	5 mL
8	slices whole wheat bread	8
	oil or nonstick cooking spray	

AT CAMP: In a shallow dish, whisk together eggs, milk and cinnamon. Place bread slices in large shallow pan; pour egg mixture over it and turn each slice to coat well. Cover and keep cool if space allows. Heat well-oiled pan on medium heat. Place as many slices in pan as possible. Cook over medium heat for 2 minutes. Turn and cook second side for 2 minutes or until golden brown. Serve with syrup.

Family-Style Granola

Margaret's family loves this homemade version of granola, which she has been making for many years, and now Kevin has adopted it for his camping trips. And who knows — maybe he'll make it at home, too!

3 cups	old-fashioned rolled oats	750 mL
1 cup	coarsely chopped pecans	250 mL
½ cup	unsweetened coconut	125 mL
2 tbsp	packed brown sugar	30 mL
½ tsp	each ground cinnamon and ginger	2 mL
¼ tsp	each ground allspice and nutmeg	1 ml
pinch	salt	pinch
⅓ cup	liquid honey	75 mL
2 tbsp	canola oil	30 mL
1 cup	assorted dried fruit	250 mL

Makes 5 cups (1.25 mL)

Preparation time:
10 minutes

Cooking time:
40 minutes

AT HOME: In a large bowl, combine rolled oats, pecans, coconut, sugar, spices and salt. Stir together the honey and oil, pour over oat mixture; stir well to distribute. Spoon onto a large parchment-lined baking sheet and bake in a 300°F (160°C) oven for about 40 minutes; stir every 10 minutes. Remove from oven and stir in dried fruit. When cool, store in a tightly sealed container for up to 1 month. Alternately, microwave mixture on High (100%) power for 3 minutes, stir and microwave for 2 more minutes. Stir well, then continue microwaving until mixture becomes slightly browned; stir after each minute. Let stand until cool; mixture will continue to brown as it cools.

Berry Good Pancakes

Any firm berry works well in this recipe. And if you happen to be near a wild blueberry patch, so much the better! This recipe works well doubled, which is especially helpful if having leftovers is desired or when feeding extra people.

¾ cup	oat or wheat bran	175 mL
½ cup	whole wheat flour	125 mL
¼ cup	ground flaxseed	60 mL
1 tbsp	each baking powder and granulated sugar	15 mL
pinch	salt	pinch
1 cup	milk	250 mL
1 tbsp	canola oil	15 mL
1	egg, beaten	1
1 cup	blueberries or mixed cranberries and blueberries	250 mL
	oil or nonstick cooking spray	

Makes 8 large pancakes

Preparation time:
10 minutes

Cooking time:
3 to 5 minutes

AT HOME: Combine bran, flour, flaxseed, baking powder, sugar and salt. Store in a tightly sealed container. If using fresh berries, carry them in a separate container and keep chilled.

AT CAMP: Place dry ingredients in a medium bowl. In a second bowl, combine milk, oil and egg and stir into dry ingredients just until blended; fold in the berries. Heat a well-oiled pan (or use nonstick cooking spray) over medium heat until hot (a drop of water will sizzle in pan). Drop batter by spoonfuls onto pan. Cook pancakes for 3 minutes or until bubbles break on top and the underside is golden brown; turn and cook second side until golden. Serve with maple syrup or Orange Maple Blueberry Sauce (page 153).

Granola Squares

½ cup	corn syrup	125 mL
2 tbsp	packed brown sugar	30 mL
⅓ cup	crunchy peanut butter	75 mL
3½ cups	Family-Style Granola (page 69)	875 mL
¼ cup	ground flaxseeds	60 mL
1 tsp	ground allspice or cinnamon	5 mL

Makes 12 squares

Preparation time:
under 10 minutes

Cooking time:
2 minutes

AT HOME: In a large container suitable for the microwave, combine syrup and sugar. Cook on High (100%) for 1½ minutes or until mixture is boiling; stir in peanut butter until smooth. Quickly stir in granola, flax-seeds and allspice until mixture is well combined. Spoon into a lightly greased 8 inch (2 L) metal pan; press down firmly. Allow to cool before cutting into squares. Store squares in a tightly sealed container.

Fruit 'n' Fiber Cookies

4	medium bananas	4
⅓ cup	canola oil	75 mL
1½ cups	large-flake rolled oats	375 mL
¾ cup	whole wheat flour	175 mL
½ cup	each dried raisins, chopped apricots, and dates	125 mL
½ cup	chopped pecans, walnuts or almonds	125 mL
	grated rind of 1 lemon	

Makes 36 cookies

Preparation time:
15 minutes

Cooking time:
20 minutes

AT HOME: In a large bowl, mash bananas. Combine bananas with oil, oats, flour, raisins, apricots, dates, nuts and lemon rind; mix well. Drop by spoon-fuls onto a greased baking sheet; flatten with a fork. Bake cookies in a 350°F (180°C) oven for 20 minutes or until cookies are golden brown. Cool completely before storing in a tightly sealed container; freeze for longer storage.

Hot Multigrain Cereal Mix

Taking ready-to-use dry cereal mix along to the campsite for a hot cereal makes an awesome start on a cold morning. If you like your hot cereal chewy, boil water first and then add cereal. If you like it creamier, combine cereal mix and water, then cook. If the serving sizes we suggest are too small, make larger amounts that will need some extra cooking time. This is always the ultimate comfort food for any morning!

1 cup	large-flake rolled oats	250 mL
1 cup	three- to seven-grain cereal	250 mL
1 cup	whole wheat flakes	250 mL
1 cup	each oat bran and ground flaxseed	250 mL

Makes 4 cups (1 L)

Preparation time:
8 minutes

Cooking time:
5 minutes

AT HOME: In a large bowl, combine rolled oats, cereal, whole wheat flakes, oat bran and flaxseed. Store in a tightly sealed container.

AT CAMP: For each serving: In a saucepan, bring ¼ cup (60 mL) cereal mix and ¾ cup (175 mL) water to a boil, reduce heat to medium-low and cook, stirring constantly, for about 5 minutes or until cereal reaches desired consistency. Cover and remove from heat. Let stand for a few minutes, then stir and serve.

VARIATIONS: Add any dried fruit you have, such as cranberries, blueberries, apples or apricots, or fresh fruit if available.

Mexican Egg-Filled Tortillas

Eggs are as important to Mexican cooking as they are to camp cooking. Fill soft tortillas with scrambled eggs and salsa. If you can, take fresh salsa rather than dried, as it is much better.

Serves 4 to 6

Preparation time:
15 minutes

Cooking time:
about 5 minutes

6	eggs	6
½ cup	milk or water	125 mL
1	small onion, chopped	1
1 tbsp	soft margarine or butter	15 mL
½ cup	grated cheese, any kind	125 mL
6	large tortillas	6
	salsa, picante or mild, your choice	
	salt and freshly ground pepper	

AT CAMP: In a bowl, combine eggs, milk, salt and pepper. In a nonstick skillet, cook onion in margarine for 5 minutes. Add egg mixture and cook over medium heat, stirring occasionally. Add cheese just before eggs are set. Warm tortillas by the fire, place on a flat surface and fill each with some of the egg mixture. Roll up and serve with salsa.

Overnight Cheese Casserole

This very easy and very tasty recipe is best made the night before. Or maybe the time to make it is when you've decided to have a lazy morning at camp.

Serves 4

Preparation time:
about 15 minutes

Cooking time:
35 minutes

6	slices whole wheat bread	6
3 cups	grated cheese, any kind	750 mL
6	eggs, beaten	6
2 cups	milk	500 mL
1	medium onion, chopped	1
1	sun-dried tomato, diced	1
	salt and freshly ground pepper	

AT CAMP: Arrange bread slices in a greased metal baking pan that will hold six slices. Sprinkle with half of the cheese. In a bowl, combine eggs, milk, onion and tomato. Pour over bread. Sprinkle with remaining cheese, salt and pepper. Cover and store in a cooler overnight. Bake in a Dutch oven (see page 55) for about 35 minutes, or until browned. Let stand for 5 minutes before cutting into squares.

Peanut Butter Banana Muffins

This is a great start to the camping day — protein from peanut butter, eggs and milk, and fruit. This is much faster than making a peanut butter and banana sandwich. Bake the muffins at home and freeze until needed, or bake in a Dutch oven at camp.

1¼ cups	all-purpose flour	300 mL
½ cup	whole wheat flour	125 mL
⅔ cup	lightly packed brown sugar	150 mL
2 tsp	baking powder	10 mL
1 tsp	ground cinnamon	5 mL
½ tsp	each baking soda and salt	2 mL
2	large bananas (about 1 cup/250 mL mashed)	2
½ cup	soft margarine or butter	125 mL
⅓ cup	peanut butter	75 mL
2	eggs (well beaten)	2
1 tsp	vanilla extract	5 mL

Makes 12 large muffins

Preparation time:
10 minutes

Cooking time:
18 minutes

AT HOME: In a large bowl, combine flours, sugar, baking powder, cinnamon, baking soda and salt. In a second bowl, combine mashed bananas, margarine, peanut butter, eggs and vanilla; stir into flour mixture just until moistened. Spoon batter into 12 nonstick or paper-lined muffin cups, filling two-thirds full. Bake in a 375°F (190°C) oven for 18 minutes, or until muffins are lightly browned and firm to the touch. Cool for 10 minutes before removing to a wire rack to cool completely. Pack in an airtight bag and freeze until needed.

AT CAMP: In a large bowl, stir mashed bananas, margarine, peanut butter, eggs and vanilla into prepared dry ingredients you brought from home. Stir just until moistened. Spoon batter into a lightly greased 8 inch (2 L) metal pan. Bake in a Dutch oven (see page 55) for 25 minutes or until muffins spring back when lightly touched and are golden brown.

Midday Meals

A few boiled eggs, some crisp cut-up raw veggies, and great bread will make the first few days of camping easy, and previously prepared homemade soups will be welcome as well. Different breads, pita, tortillas, cornbread and a variety of crackers and cheeses will also get lunches off to quick starts. For later in the trip when the ice melts, build lunches with quinoa, pasta or beans. We always suggest that as much planning goes into this meal as any other, even though it is usually a short stop on a day's journey. This preplanning takes place at home, with menus planned, items measured out and properly labeled, and extra care taken when shopping, as we want to carry as few items as possible. But the better equipped your camp is, the more elaborate your meals can be.

Borscht in Minutes

This is certainly one of the easiest recipes we have ever used for this traditional beet soup. Either make it at home or carry the few ingredients along with you. Chilled sour cream will keep for several days, as will yogurt. If this is too much to carry, the soup is still wonderful without it.

Serves 3 to 4

Preparation time:
about 10 minutes

Cooking time:
10 minutes

1	small onion, chopped	1
1 tbsp	soft margarine or butter	15 mL
1 can	(19 oz/540 mL) beets with juice	1 can
1 cup	broth or water	250 mL
1 tbsp	horseradish	15 mL
	salt and freshly ground pepper	
	sour cream or plain yogurt (optional)	

AT HOME: In small pan, sauté the onion in melted margarine for 5 minutes or until soft. In blender, purée the onions and beets with the juice, broth and horseradish until very smooth. Season with salt and pepper to taste. Store in a tightly sealed container and refrigerate, or freeze for longer storage.

AT CAMP: Thaw beet mixture, cook over medium heat until hot. Serve with a dollop of sour cream or yogurt, if available.

Cheesy Macaroni

Here is a fast take on that good old standby, mac 'n' cheese. Time will be available the night before, so plan on cooking extra macaroni to use the next day. When shopping, remember to buy a package of grated cheese (see the Camp Tip). The cheese needs to be kept cold, so this may become one of those lunches you enjoy early in the trip.

1 tbsp	soft margarine or butter	15 mL	Serves 2
½	small onion, chopped	½	
1 tbsp	all-purpose flour	15 mL	**Preparation time:** 10 minutes
¾ cup	milk	175 mL	
1 cup	grated cheese, any kind (Cheddar is preferred)	250 mL	**Cooking time:** 10 minutes
Pinch	each dry mustard, salt, freshly ground pepper	Pinch	
2 cups	cooked elbow macaroni	500 mL	

AT CAMP: In skillet, melt margarine, add onion and cook on medium for 5 minutes or until onion is tender. Stir in flour and milk; continue stirring until thickened. Add cheese, stir until melted, stir in cooked macaroni and cook just until heated. Season to taste with mustard, salt and pepper.

CAMP TIP: Wrap the cheese in cheesecloth soaked in vinegar — this will help cheese to stay fresh longer.

Dilled Bean and Tomato Salad

This salad makes a hearty and very easy lunch to serve with buns or bannock bread. It fills up the empty spaces after a morning on the trail or a portage. Much of this recipe can be prepared at home, but definitely remove the beans and tomatoes from their cans before storing them in tightly sealed containers.

Dressing

Serves 4

Preparation time:
15 minutes

¼ cup	olive oil	60 mL
2 tbsp	fresh lemon juice	30 mL
1 tbsp	balsamic vinegar	15 mL
	chopped fresh or dried dill	

Salad

2	cans (19 oz/540 mL) kidney beans, drained	2
2 cups	canned chopped tomatoes, drained	500 mL
⅔ cup	diced red onion	150 mL
	salt and freshly ground pepper	

AT HOME: Combine olive oil, lemon juice and balsamic vinegar. Store in tightly sealed container. Open cans of kidney beans and tomatoes, store in tightly sealed containers.

AT CAMP: In large bowl, toss drained kidney beans, tomatoes and onion. Stir in olive oil mixture. Season to taste with salt and pepper. Cover and marinate at room temperature for 1 hour.

It's possible to dine on fresh sprouts halfway through a trip. On day one or two, soak beans or seeds in water for half a day and then store them in a plastic bottle capped with a thin cloth held on with an elastic band. Other than being rinsed with water daily, they need little care. On day five or six (depending on the temperature), you'll have a fresh additive for dinners or lunches — sprouts. Alfalfa sprouts are the easiest to work with, mustard seeds add a great zip, and garbanzo beans (chickpeas) and green lentils have the most flavor. Just make sure to take the sprouts into the tent with you if it gets cold at night.

Hot Diggity Dog Tomato Soup

By using wieners and pasta in this soup, you are assured of a winning combination for children's lunches

1	pkg (2.5 oz/71 g) dried tomato soup	1
4 cups	water or milk	1 L
½ cup	dry elbow macaroni	125 mL
4	wieners, sliced diagonally	4
	grated Parmesan cheese	

Serves 3 to 4

Preparation time: about 5 minutes

Cooking time: 10 minutes

AT CAMP: In a medium saucepan, combine soup, water or milk, then bring to boil. Add macaroni and cook for 5 minutes. Add wieners, cook for another 5 minutes. Sprinkle with cheese when serving.

Mexican Bean Tacos

Beans are an essential part of Mexican cuisine, and they can also have a place in outdoor camping cuisine. If you are carrying a large thermos and have the stove on for breakfast, this mixture can be heated and kept in the thermos for lunch.

1	medium onion, chopped	1
2	garlic cloves, minced	2
2 tbsp	soft margarine or butter	30 mL
1	can (19 oz/540 mL) beans in tomato sauce	1
1 tsp	each: cumin and chili powder	5 mL
8	crisp taco shells	8
	grated Cheddar cheese	
	chopped tomatoes and shredded lettuce (optional)	

Serves 4

Preparation time: 15 minutes

Cooking time: 10 minutes

AT HOME: Measure cumin and chili powder and store in small tightly sealed container. Remove beans from can and store in tightly sealed container.

AT CAMP: In nonstick skillet, cook onion and garlic in melted margarine until soft. Stir in beans and seasonings, simmer over medium heat until hot; stir frequently. Warm taco shells, spoon hot bean mixture into shells, top with cheese, tomato and lettuce, if using them.

Huevos Rancheros

This is a Mexican classic suitable for a rainy day at the campsite. Liquid eggs, which come in a variety of flavors and can be frozen, make this Mexican-inspired lunch even easier. A salad or cooked rice would finish this easy menu item.

Serves 2 to 4

Preparation time:
about 5 minutes

Cooking time:
15 minutes

1	small onion, chopped	1
¼ cup	chopped sweet green pepper	60 mL
1 tbsp	soft margarine or butter	15 mL
2 cups	canned chopped tomatoes, drained	500 mL
2 tsp	chili powder	10 mL
1 tsp	garlic powder	5 mL
½ tsp	each salt and pepper	2 mL
4	eggs or 1 cup (250 mL) liquid eggs	4
4	large whole wheat tortillas	4

AT HOME: Measure chili and garlic powders, salt and pepper and store in a small, tightly sealed container.

AT CAMP: In a nonstick skillet, cook onion and green pepper in margarine for 5 minutes. Add tomatoes and seasonings and simmer for 10 minutes. Break each egg into tomato mixture, cover and cook on medium heat until eggs are set, about 5 minutes. (Or pour liquid eggs over tomato mixture and proceed as with whole eggs.) Warm tortillas; serve eggs with sauce over tortillas.

CAMP TIP: If using dehydrated green pepper and tomatoes, add up to ½ cup (125 mL) water in skillet to rehydrate vegetables.

Mushroom Quinoa Salad

Since quinoa is rich in plant fat, like nuts, it spoils easily. Store in an airtight glass container no longer than one month, or in the refrigerator or freezer for longer storage. Quinoa is widely available in bulk food stores and supermarkets.

	Salt and freshly ground pepper	
1 cup	quinoa	250 mL
2 cups	broth or water	500 mL
1 tbsp	canola or olive oil	15 mL
2	💧 small carrots, grated	2
1	💧 sweet red pepper, diced	1
1 cup	💧 sliced mushrooms	250 mL
2	garlic cloves, minced	¼ cup

Serves 4

Preparation time:
15 minutes

Cooking time:
about 20 minutes

Dressing

4 tbsp	rice vinegar	60 mL
3 tbsp	soy sauce	45 mL
1 tbsp	grated fresh gingerroot	15 mL
1 tsp	sesame oil	5 mL

AT HOME: Combine vinegar, soy sauce, gingerroot, sesame oil, salt and pepper. Store in a tightly sealed container.

AT CAMP: Rinse quinoa under cold water until water runs clear. In medium saucepan, bring broth to a boil; add the quinoa to broth, cover, reduce heat and simmer for 15 minutes or until grains are translucent. Remove from the heat. Fluff with a fork and let stand for 15 minutes.

IF USING DEHYDRATED VEGETABLES: Add these to the quinoa with the broth. You may require more broth for full rehydration. When quinoa is translucent, stir in the dressing. Serve warm.

IF USING FRESH VEGETABLES: In nonstick skillet on medium heat, heat oil; add carrots, red pepper, mushrooms and garlic; cook for 5 minutes or until vegetables are tender. Remove from heat, stir in dressing. Serve warm.

Quinoa Tabbouleh

Tabbouleh, from the Middle East, is normally made using bulgur (cracked wheat), but for a change, as well as for higher quality protein, here we offer a version using quinoa. Furthermore, using quinoa makes the recipe gluten-free. The salad will benefit if the dressing can be added and left for about 1 hour. We like it best when served at room temperature. Take it on your morning activity to enjoy for a quick lunch.

Salad

Makes about 5 cups
(1.25 L)

Cooking time:
12 minutes

1 cup	quinoa	250 mL
½ cup	water	125 mL
1 cup	◊ chopped parsley	250 mL
1 cup	◊ diced cucumber	250 mL
2	green onions, chopped	2
½ cup	◊ diced sweet red pepper	125 mL
¼ cup	chopped fresh mint	60 mL
	or 1 tbsp (15 mL) dried mint	

Dressing

3 tbsp	fresh lemon juice or white wine vinegar	45 mL
2 tbsp	olive or canola oil	30 mL
	salt and freshly ground pepper	

AT HOME: Combine lemon juice and oil. Store in tightly sealed container.

AT CAMP: Salad: Rinse quinoa under cold running water until water runs clear. In saucepan, bring ½ cup (125 mL) water to a boil; add quinoa, reduce heat, cover and simmer for 15 minutes or until the grains are translucent. Remove from heat, fluff with fork and let stand for 15 minutes. Cool, add parsley, cucumber, onions, red pepper and mint.

DRESSING: Stir prepared dressing into the quinoa mixture; season to taste with salt and pepper.

Pasta and Green Pea Salad with Red Onion

In the morning, cook the pasta, adding peas during last couple of minutes; cool slightly. Makes a fast and tasty lunch meal.

1	pkg (12 oz/375 g) fusilli or rotini pasta	1
2 cups	💧 green peas	500 mL
1	small red onion, chopped	1
	freshly grated Parmesan cheese	
	salt, freshly ground pepper, olive oil to taste	

Serves 3 to 4

Preparation time:
15 minutes

Cooking time:
7–9 minutes

In a large pot of boiling water, cook pasta according to package directions, about 8 minutes or until al dente; drain well. During last few minutes add peas, drain and cool. Add onion, cheese, salt, pepper and olive oil to taste. Pack in a suitable container to take on the morning outing.

Penne Pesto with Tuna

Fast and easy? You bet — this dish comes together in no time. Again, this recipe may be enjoyed on a lazy day or it can be cooked at breakfast and taken with you on the morning activity — it is delicious even when cold!

1	pkg (1 lb/450 g) penne	1
2	pkgs (3 oz/85 g each) tuna	2
⅔ cup	Pesto sauce	150 mL
1	large tomato, chopped	1
2	green onions, chopped (optional)	2
	or chopped dried chives	

Serves 4

Preparation time:
5 minutes

Cooking time:
15 minutes

AT CAMP: In large pot of boiling water, cook penne according to package directions, about 8 minutes or until al dente; drain well. Return to the pot, stir in tuna, pesto, tomato and onions until combined.

Rice Scrambled Eggs

Leftovers — what to do with them? When it comes to cooked rice, just add it to eggs and do a fast scramble for lunch. Liquid eggs make this lunch even easier. How simple is this? There's no need for toast, either!

Serves 2

Preparation time:
5 minutes

Cooking time:
5 minutes

1 tbsp	soft margarine or butter	15 mL
4	eggs or 1 cup (250 mL) liquid eggs	4
1 cup	cold cooked rice	250 mL
¼ cup	milk	60 mL
	salt, pepper and hot sauce (all optional)	

AT CAMP: In a nonstick skillet, melt margarine over medium to low heat. Combine eggs, rice, milk, as well as the salt, pepper and hot sauce, if desired. Pour into skillet and cook, stirring frequently, until eggs are cooked to desired consistency.

Salmon Sandwiches

By always having a couple of cans or packages of tuna, salmon or even sardines, sandwiches can be easily made at breakfast to take for lunch.

Salmon Filling:

Serves 2

Preparation time:
10 minutes

1	pkg (3 oz/ 85 g) salmon	1
2 tbsp	yogurt	30 mL
1 tbsp	vinegar	15 mL
1 tbsp	chopped onion	15 mL
	chopped nuts, salt and freshly ground pepper, to taste	
	soft margarine or butter	
4	slices whole wheat bread or bannock	4

AT CAMP: In bowl, flake salmon. Add yogurt, vinegar, onion, nuts, salt and pepper. Spread margarine on bread slices, top 2 slices with salmon filling and close sandwich.

Ruth's Onion Pie

My good friend Ruth recently served this pie for lunch to Margaret, who immediately asked for the recipe, as it is simple and can be easily adapted for an outdoor brunch or lunch.

2 cups	cracker crumbs	500 mL	Serves 4
½ cup	melted soft margarine or butter, divided	125 mL	**Preparation time:**
3 cups	thinly sliced sweet white onions	750 mL	15 minutes
3	eggs or ¾ cup (175 mL) liquid eggs	3	
1 cup	milk	250 mL	**Cooking time:**
¼ tsp	each salt and freshly ground pepper	1 mL	about 20 minutes
½ cup	grated sharp Cheddar cheese	125 mL	

AT HOME: Prepare the crumbs and store them in a tightly sealed container.

AT CAMP: Combine crumbs with one-half of melted margarine. Press into a metal pie plate to form a shell.

In large nonstick skillet, sauté onions in the remaining margarine for a few minutes or until they are soft. Spoon onions over crumbs.

In bowl, combine eggs, milk, salt and pepper. Pour over onions, sprinkle with cheese, bake in Dutch oven (see page 55) for about 20 minutes or until center is set. Cut into 4 wedges and serve.

Salmon Vegetable Casserole

A meal in a dish! This is a great way, near the end of a camping trip, to use up bits and pieces of dehydrated veggies and some cheese. With smoked salmon, this will be an award-winning meal.

Serves 2 to 3

Preparation time:
12 minutes

Cooking time:
about 20 minutes

1	pkg (5½ oz/ 150 g) smoked salmon	1
1	small zucchini, thinly sliced	1
½ cup	peas	125 mL
1 cup	grated mozzarella cheese	250 mL
¼ cup	mayonnaise	60 mL
2	eggs	2
½	small chopped onion	½
Pinch	dried dill weed	Pinch
Pinch	freshly ground pepper	Pinch

AT CAMP: Mash salmon with a fork, add zucchini, peas, cheese, mayonnaise, eggs, onion, dill weed and pepper. Stir to combine. Pour mixture into greased medium foil casserole dish. Bake in a Dutch oven (see page 55) and bake for 35 minutes or until it is heated and set in the center.

Tuna Quesadilla

When you fill soft flour tortillas with a cheese, meat or fish mixture and then fold the tortilla over, it is called a *quesadilla*. Include in the filling either cooked or canned fish, meats, vegetables, refried beans or all of the above (except perhaps for the meat if you are using fish). Monterey Jack or mozzarella are good melting cheeses to use. And there is nothing wrong with enjoying the quesadillas cold, except that the cheese will not be melted.

4	large flour or whole wheat tortillas	4
½ cup	grated cheese	125 mL
1	pkg (3 oz/ 85 g) tuna	1
	salsa: mild, medium or hot	

Serves 2

Preparation time:
10 minutes

Cooking time:
5 minutes

AT CAMP: Place tortillas on a flat surface. In bowl, combine cheese, tuna and enough salsa to moisten the ingredients so they will hold together. Divide mixture over surface of 2 tortillas, spreading to edge. Top with remaining 2 tortillas, and press the edges to seal the tortillas. Heat a large nonstick skillet over medium-high heat. Cook them one at a time, turning them in order to brown both sides. Remove the first quesadilla from pan, cut it into wedges and enjoy while the next quesadilla is cooking.

Quick Pickups

No matter how tired you are, great snacks during the day and appetizers to anticipate before dinner will give you those extra calories needed to refuel. Most of the recipes in this chapter are easy to make at home, thus taking the work out of a camping day, and many will survive the trip without refrigeration. The Nacho Cheese 'n' Salsa Appetizer is made at camp, but since this recipe only has three ingredients, go for it. Of course you will want to make the bannock fresh. Lots of fresh veggies will be welcome the first few days out for dipping and feasting.

Apricot Sunflower Seed Cereal Bars

Crisp and chewy, this bar is a good-for-you alternative to store-bought cereal bars. The secret ingredient is yogurt, which will give your day a protein-packed start. This recipe will work with many other fruit and nuts or seed combinations.

Makes 32 bars

Preparation time:
15 minutes

Cooking time:
40 minutes

2 cups	large-flake rolled oats	500 mL
½ cup	sunflower seeds	125 mL
3 cups	puffed or crispy rice cereal	750 mL
2 cups	chopped dried apricots	500 mL
¼ cup	whole wheat flour	60 mL
½ tsp	salt	2 mL
1	tub (17.6 oz/500 g) Greek-style vanilla yogurt	1
1	egg	1
⅓ cup	canola oil	75 mL
1 cup	liquid honey	250 mL
	zest of 1 lemon	
1 tsp	vanilla extract	5 mL
	oil or nonstick cooking spray	

AT HOME: Grease a large jelly-roll style baking sheet with oil or cooking spray. Spread oats and sunflower seeds on the pan, bake in 350°F (180°C) oven for 8 to 10 minutes, or until golden brown. Transfer to a large bowl, stir in cereal, apricots, flour and salt until well mixed.

Meanwhile, purée yogurt, egg, oil, honey, lemon zest and vanilla in a food processor or blender until smooth. Make a well in the center of the dried mixture, pour in liquid and stir well to combine. Spread evenly on baking sheet. Bake in oven for 35 minutes or until firm in the center and golden brown. Let cool completely in the pan on a wire rack before cutting into bars with a sharp knife. Make ahead of the trip, wrap each bar in plastic and keep at room temperature for 5 days or freeze for longer storage.

Basic Bannock and Variations

Kevin has been using this recipe since his early camping days, so why improve on perfection? Since this bread has no yeast, no kneading is required. The best way to eat this is to tear the bannock apart and spread it with margarine or butter and jam or honey and then devour it.

½ cup	all-purpose flour	125 mL
½ cup	whole wheat flour	125 mL
3 tbsp	powdered milk	45 mL
1 tsp	baking powder	5 mL
½ tsp	salt	2 mL
¼ cup	water	60 mL
	canola oil	

Makes 3 to 4 patties

Preparation time:
5 minutes

Cooking time:
about 2 minutes per side

AT HOME: Combine flours, powdered milk, baking powder and salt. Store in a tightly sealed container.

AT CAMP: In a small bowl, combine dry ingredients with water, adding water slowly until dough gets slightly sticky. Divide into three to four patties. Add a small amount of oil to a heavy skillet, heat over medium heat, add patties and cook evenly so the center is done, about 2 minutes per side or until brown, turning several times during cooking. Check bannock to see if it is cooked through by poking a skewer in the center. As a change to cooking the bannock as patties, try wrapping it around a 2-inch (5 cm) thick stick. Pinch dough to seal, then cook over hot coals.

VARIATIONS: Add sunflower or sesame seeds, raisins, and dried cranberries with cinnamon, or any other spice to create a less-bland bannock. Kevin's final tip is to add a teaspoon of rum when the second side is being cooked — it makes a huge difference to the taste!

Bran Muffins

Bake these muffins at home and freeze until needed, or bake in a Dutch oven at camp.

Makes 12 large muffins

Preparation time:
10 minutes

Cooking time:
18 minutes

1½ cups	natural bran	375 mL
1½ cups	whole wheat flour	375 mL
1¼ cups	all-purpose flour	300 mL
2 tsp	each baking powder and baking soda	10 mL
½ tsp	salt	2 mL
¾ cup	soft margarine or butter	175 mL
⅔ cup	lightly packed brown sugar	150 mL
2 cups	◖ buttermilk	500 mL
½ cup	raisins	125 mL
¼ cup	molasses	60 mL
2	◖ eggs, well beaten	2

To prepare for cooking at camp: In a large bowl, combine bran, flours, baking powder, baking soda and salt. Store in a tightly sealed container. In a second bowl, cream the margarine and brown sugar. Add buttermilk, raisins and molasses; stir in eggs. Store in a tightly sealed container and refrigerate, or freeze for longer storage.

AT HOME: In a large bowl, stir liquid mixture into flour mixture, stirring just until moistened. Spoon batter into 12 nonstick or paper-lined large muffin cups, filling two-thirds full. Bake in a 400°F (200°C) oven for 18 minutes, or until muffins are lightly browned and firm to the touch. Cool for 10 minutes before removing from tins to wire rack to cool completely. Pack in airtight container and freeze until needed.

AT CAMP: Bring prepared dry ingredients and liquid from home. Thaw liquid mixture if made at home, or prepare it at camp. Pre-heat a Dutch oven (see page 55). In a large bowl, prepare muffin mixture as above, adding liquid ingredients to dry; spoon batter into prepared muffin pan. Bake muffins for 18 minutes or until lightly browned and firm to the touch.

Corn 'n' Black Bean Salsa

This salsa is wonderful for hearty scooping with nachos or corn tortillas. It's also nice served with grilled pork chops or tenderloin

2 cups	corn niblets	500 mL	Makes 3 cups (750 mL)
1 cup	cooked black beans	250 mL	
⅓ cup	chopped fresh or 1 tbsp (15 mL) dried parsley	75 mL	**Preparation time:** 15 minutes
¼ cup	finely chopped red onion	60 mL	
3 tbsp	each fresh lime juice and olive oil	45 mL	
	hot sauce, salt and freshly ground pepper, to taste		

AT HOME. Combine corn, beans, parsley, onion, lime juice, oil, hot sauce, salt and pepper to taste; mix well. Store in a tightly covered container and refrigerate for up to four days.

CAMP TIP: This salsa is better not frozen, but is easy to assemble at the campsite. Canned beans, drained and rinsed, replace having to cook dry beans. And canned corn works just fine. Or use dehydrated vegetables and reconstitute them.

LEFT Nachos are an excellent choice to pair with this delicious salsa recipe.

Creamy Apple Cheese Spread

Serve this spread either as a quick lunch or at snack time for crackers or apple slices. To store, spoon into several small containers, refrigerate or freeze, and remove as needed. See the Camp Tip if you plan to replace mayonnaise with dehydrated yogurt and cream cheese with cottage cheese.

Makes 1½ cups (375 mL)

Preparation time:
10 minutes

Chill time:
2 hours

1	pkg (8 oz/225 g) cream cheese (see Camp Tip)	1
1 cup	shredded Cheddar cheese	250 mL
¼ cup	mayonnaise (see Camp Tip)	60 mL
1 tbsp	fresh lemon juice	15 mL
¼ tsp	dry mustard	1 mL
2	medium apples	2

AT HOME: In a small bowl, beat cream cheese with an immersion blender or a food processor until smooth. Beat in Cheddar cheese, mayonnaise, lemon juice and mustard until creamy. Store spread in several tightly sealed containers in the refrigerator, or freeze for longer storage.

AT CAMP: Remove spread from cooler or thaw if frozen; let stand at room temperature for 15 minutes to become soft enough for spreading. Core, peel and slice apples. Spread with cheese mixture.

CAMP TIPS: Prepare only as many apple slices as are needed. Keep spread cool to use later (if those hungry campers leave any). To make this dip at camp, bring dehydrated 1% plain yogurt and 1% cottage cheese from home as a replacement for mayonnaise and cream cheese. Dehydrated yogurt is best kept refrigerated and will last for up to 6 months, or can be stored at room temperature for up to a week. If using dehydrated yogurt and cottage cheese, rehydrate them with either a small amount of water or milk and then stir the yogurt, cottage cheese, Cheddar cheese, mayonnaise, lemon juice and mustard until creamy.

Hearty Rolled Oat Cookies

These cookies are a great camping treat when a fast pick-me-up
is needed on the trail. They have a high fiber count and are real
energy boosters due to their high calorie content.

1⅓ cups	canola oil	325 mL
1 cup	each brown and granulated sugar	250 mL
2	large eggs	2
2 tsp	vanilla extract	10 mL
4 cups	large-flake rolled oats	1 L
2 cups	whole wheat flour	500 mL
2 tsp	each baking powder and baking soda	10 mL
1 tsp	each ground cinnamon and salt	5 mL

Makes 3 dozen cookies

Preparation time:
15 minutes

Cooking time:
10 minutes

AT HOME: In a large bowl, beat the oil, sugars, eggs and vanilla
until smooth. In a medium bowl, combine rolled oats, flour, baking
powder, baking soda, cinnamon and salt. Stir flour mixture into oil
mixture. Drop dough by spoonfuls onto greased baking sheets;
flatten each with a fork. Bake in a 350°F (180°C) oven for 10 minutes or until cookies are golden brown and crisp at the edges.
Transfer to a rack to cool. Store cookies in a tightly sealed container for up to five days, or freeze for longer storage.

CAMP TIP: We added chocolate chips to half of the batter, but they
really are still delicious without them. Dried cranberries or raisins
are a nice addition as well.

Homemade Energy Bars

Many times we have eaten commercial energy bars, but decided for this book to give you a recipe to make at home. It has now become a favorite enjoyed by all. We hope it becomes a favorite of yours as well.

Makes 36 to 40 bars

Preparation time:
10 minutes

Cooking time:
15 minutes

1 cup	packed brown sugar	250 mL
½ cup	soft margarine or butter	125 mL
¼ cup	liquid honey	60 mL
⅔ cup	peanut butter (see Cooking Tip)	150 mL
2 tsp	vanilla extract	10 mL
3 cups	rolled oats	750 mL
1 cup	sliced almonds	250 mL
1 cup	dried fruit (see Cooking Tip)	250 mL
¼ cup	chocolate chips	60 mL

AT HOME: In a large bowl, beat sugar with margarine until smooth. Add honey, peanut butter and vanilla; beat until well blended. Stir in rolled oats, almonds, dried fruit and chocolate chips. Press into a greased 9x13 inch (3.5 L) baking pan. Bake in a 350°F (180°C) oven for 15 minutes or until brown around the edges and the center is firm. Remove pan from oven and cool slightly before cutting into whatever size bars you wish. Store in resealable plastic bags or wrap tightly with plastic — they travel well.

COOKING TIP: When there is a peanut allergy, replace peanut butter with almond butter. There are many dried fruit choices — raisins, blueberries, cherries, cranberries, apples, mangos or pear slices (you may want to cut these into smaller pieces with scissors).

Lentil Dip

Much like hummus, this new take on the popular vegetable dip is sufficiently different that it makes a nice alternative to hummus. Strictly according to the dictionary, lentils are called pulses. They are high in fiber, complex carbohydrates, protein, B-vitamins and potassium. Raw veggies or crisp tortillas make the best dippers. Naturally, bouillon cubes will be used to make the broth, any flavor you prefer.

½ cup	dried red lentils, rinsed and drained	125 mL
1½ cups	water	375 mL
1 to 2	chicken or vegetable bouillon cubes	1 to 2
1	small clove garlic, sliced	1
2 tsp	olive oil	10 mL
1 tsp	fresh lemon juice	5 mL
¼ tsp	dry mustard	1 mL
	salt and freshly ground pepper to taste	

Makes 1⅓ cups (325 mL)

Preparation time:
15 minutes

Cooking time:
10 minutes

AT HOME: In a medium saucepan, cook lentils, water and bouillon cubes for 10 minutes or until lentils are tender (do not overcook, as they become mushy). Drain immediately. In a food processor or blender, purée lentils, garlic, oil, lemon juice and mustard until mixture is smooth. Add salt and pepper to taste. Store in a tightly sealed container and refrigerate, or freeze for longer storage.

CAMP TIP: This dip tastes even better when served warm with tortillas.

Logan Bread

We have found several recipes for this type of bread named after Mt. Logan in the Yukon. It is a quick bread full of dried fruits and nuts. High in calories and full of nutrients, this bread is perfect for hiking and camping. Don't restrict yourself to just raisins and sunflower seeds — use almonds, walnuts, dried cranberries or anything you fancy to add a little more zest!

Makes 36 servings

Preparation time:
15 minutes

Cooking time:
45 minutes

1½ cups	whole wheat flour	375 mL
1½ cups	unbleached all-purpose flour	375 mL
1¼ cups	rolled oats	300 mL
¾ cup	lightly packed brown sugar	175 mL
1½ tsp	baking powder	7 mL
1 tsp	salt	5 mL
2	eggs	2
1 cup	applesauce	250 mL
½ cup	liquid honey	125 mL
½ cup	canola oil	125 mL
¼ cup	molasses	60 mL
1 cup	raisins	250 mL
⅔ cup	sunflower seeds	150 mL

AT HOME: In a large bowl, combine flours, rolled oats, sugar, baking powder and salt. In a second bowl, stir together eggs, applesauce, honey, oil and molasses. Pour liquid ingredients into dry ingredients; stir just until well blended. Stir in raisins and sunflower seeds. Divide batter into two greased 9-inch (23 cm) square pans. Bake in a 350°F (180°C) oven for 45 minutes or until the top springs back when lightly pressed. Remove from oven; allow to cool in pans for 10 minutes before cutting into squares or bars. Wrap pieces individually and refrigerate, or freeze for longer storage.

CAMP TIP: Kie successfully varied the recipe based on what ingredients she traveled with. "I didn't use all-purpose flour, applesauce (had none), or molasses (had none, very nutritious). Instead: 3 cups whole wheat flour, 1 cup honey and 1 cup oil." And it worked fine!

Nacho, Cheese 'n' Salsa Appetizer

When we have served this appetizer, our camping friends absolutely grab it by the handful! Only three ingredients — how simple does it get? Either take fresh salsa from home or dehydrate it for longer storage.

1	large bag nacho chips	1
2 cups	grated cheese, any kind	500 mL
½ cup	salsa (mild, medium or hot)	125 mL

AT CAMP: Place nachos in a large metal pan; evenly top with cheese and salsa. Place near an open fire or other heat source, but not right on the fire. Keep a close watch and cook only until cheese has melted, becoming wonderfully gooey, and nachos are held together by the cheese and salsa. Yummy!

Serves 6 hungry people

Preparation time:
5 minutes

Cooking time:
about 10 minutes

Pesto Polenta Appetizer Pie

Polenta, a cornmeal comfort food from northern Italy, is available in tubes in the deli section of the supermarket. When sliced it makes an ideal base for this appetizer pie.

1	roll (1 lb/500 g) polenta	1
½ cup	finely chopped sun-dried tomatoes	125 mL
½ cup	prepared pesto sauce (see Camp Tip)	125 mL
1 cup	shredded cheese (any kind)	250 mL

AT CAMP: Thinly slice polenta into 18 slices. Arrange 9 in the bottom of a metal baking pan. Top them with tomatoes and a dollop of pesto sauce, spreading evenly over slices. Firmly press remaining polenta slices over pesto. Sprinkle with cheese, cover with foil and place pan on a grill or over a Coleman stove on medium-low heat. Bake for about 10 minutes, or until polenta is heated and cheese melted.

CAMP TIP: Pesto sauce comes in many different-sized bottles at the grocery store and keeps well without refrigeration.

Serves 9

Preparation time:
10 minutes

Cooking time:
about 10 minutes

Tex-Mex Mix

Three simple ingredients are all you need!

Makes 4 cups (1 L)

Preparation time:
10 minutes

Cooking time:
10 minutes

4 cups	unsweetened cereal	1 L
⅓ cup	melted soft margarine or butter	75 mL
1	pkg (1.25 oz/35 g) taco seasoning mix	1

AT HOME OR AT CAMP: In a large bowl, combine cereal, margarine and taco mix; toss well to coat. Spread on a large baking pan, bake in a 350°F (180°C) oven for about 10 minutes; stir once partway through (see Camp Tip). Allow to cool before storing in a tightly sealed container.

CAMP TIP: At camp, place in a Dutch oven (see page 55) or near the campfire. Allow to become lightly browned.

Cajun Roasted Chickpeas

One of our most flavorful snacks, this one also benefits by being low in saturated fats. It's great for munching on as you walk the trail.

Makes 2 cups (500 mL)

Preparation time:
5 minutes

Cooking time:
35 minutes

2 tbsp	canola oil	30 mL
2 tsp	Cajun seasoning	10 mL
¼ tsp	each salt, garlic powder and cumin	1 mL
1	can (19 oz/540 mL) chickpeas	1

AT HOME: In a large bowl, stir together oil, Cajun seasoning, salt, garlic powder and cumin. Drain and rinse chickpeas, pat dry with paper towels. Stir into oil mixture until well coated. Spread on a large baking sheet and bake in a 400°F (200°C) oven for 35 minutes or until crisp and dried. Allow to cool before storing in a tightly sealed container.

Gourmet Trail Mix

Yes, we mean gourmet. Everyone loves this very flavorful combination.

1 cup	slivered blanched almonds	250 mL	Makes 4 cups (1 L)
½ cup	sunflower seeds	125 mL	
1 cup	flaked coconut	250 mL	**Preparation time:** 10 minutes
½ cup	dried cranberries	125 mL	
½ cup	chopped dried apricots	125 mL	**Cooking time:**
½ cup	chocolate chips	125 mL	5 minutes

AT HOME! On a large baking sheet, spread almonds and sunflower seeds and bake in a 350°F (180°C) oven for 10 minutes. Allow to cool. Meanwhile, spread coconut on a baking sheet. Reduce oven to 250°F (120°C) and bake for 5 minutes or until golden brown; cool. In a large bowl, toss almond mixture, coconut, cranberries, apricots and chocolate chips; toss well to combine. Store in a tightly sealed container.

Snappy Red Pepper Dip

This easy-to-make dip is great served with raw veggies or bread sticks. Crisp corn tortillas are also excellent.

1	bottle (10 oz/300 mL) sweet red peppers	1	Makes 1 cup (250 mL)
1	large clove garlic	1	
¼ cup	light mayonnaise or 1% yogurt	60 mL	**Preparation time:** 10 minutes
2 tbsp	chopped fresh or 1 tsp (5 mL) dried basil	30 mL	
dash	hot pepper sauce	dash	
	salt and freshly ground pepper, to taste		

AT HOME: Drain liquid from peppers. In a blender or food processor, purée red peppers, garlic and mayonnaise until smooth. Stir in basil, hot pepper sauce, salt and pepper to taste. Remove to a tightly sealed container, cover, and refrigerate for up to one week, or freeze for longer storage.

10

Dinners

We all know that it is essential to eat well while camping and that, having said that, food always seems to taste better when it is cooked outside, and when you have worked up an appetite! When is that more important than at the end of a tripping day? Tired as you are, we believe these sumptuous recipes will be an inspiration to you.

Baked Lentils and Brown Rice

When you have leftover cooked rice, here is a fine use for it the next day. You can also cook the rice and lentils just before making this recipe. The Mustard-Glazed Tomatoes (see next page) make the perfect vegetarian companion to this recipe.

½ cup	long grain brown rice (see Cooking Times)	125 mL	Serves 2
½ cup	red lentils (see Cooking Times)	125 mL	
1 cup	grated Cheddar cheese, divided	250 mL	**Preparation time:** 15 minutes
½ cup	finely shredded carrots	125 mL	
¼ cup	milk	60 mL	**Cooking time:**
2	eggs, beaten	2	30 minutes
1	small onion, chopped	1	
	salt and freshly ground black pepper to taste		
¼ cup	diced sun-dried tomatoes	60 mL	

AT CAMP: In a medium saucepan, add the rice to 1 cup (250 mL) boiling water, return to a boil, reduce heat, cover and cook for 25 minutes or until the rice is tender: drain. In a medium saucepan, add dry lentils to 1½ cups (375 mL) boiling water, return to a boil, reduce heat, cover and cook for 10 minutes or until lentils are tender; drain. In a large bowl, combine the cooked rice, lentils, ½ cup (125 mL) cheese, carrots, milk, eggs, onion, salt and pepper. Stir well and spoon into a large, lightly greased metal baking dish. Place the pan in a Dutch oven (see page 55). Bake for 30 minutes or until the mixture is set. Remove from oven, top with remaining cheese and tomatoes.

COOKING TIMES:

Long-grain brown rice: 25 to 30 minutes
Short-grain brown rice: 40 minutes
Long-grain white rice: 20 minutes
Converted rice: 31 minutes
Red lentils: about 10 minutes
Green lentils: 35 minutes
½ cup dry red lentils = 1 cup (250 mL) cooked

Mustard-Glazed Tomatoes

Fast and easy, these tomatoes are a perfect side dish for the first or second night out.

Serves 2

Preparation time:
10 minutes

Cooking time:
20 minutes

4	large tomatoes	4
½ tsp	each salt and dried thyme	2 mL
2 tbsp	each brown sugar and Dijon mustard	30 mL
2 tbsp	soft margarine or butter	30 mL

Cut a thin slice from the top of each tomato. Using a small knife, make a cross-cut on the top of each tomato about 1 inch (2.5 cm) deep. Place the tomato cut-side up in a small foil baking dish. Stir together the salt, thyme, sugar and mustard; spread mixture evenly on top of tomatoes. Dot each with margarine. Bake on either a camp stove or directly on the barbecue grill for about 20 minutes, or until tomatoes soften and are heated through.

Barley Risotto with Vegetables

Barley stands in for rice in this version of risotto. This is a great source of fiber, and is hugely flavorful!

Serves 4

Preparation time:
10 minutes

Cooking time:
about 40 minutes

1 tbsp	canola oil or olive oil	15 mL
1	medium onion, finely chopped	1
1	clove garlic, minced	1
1	medium carrot, grated	1
¼ cup	chopped red sweet pepper	60 mL
½ cup	pearl barley	125 mL
2 cups	water	500 mL
2	chicken bouillon cubes	2
	freshly ground black pepper	

AT CAMP: In a medium saucepan, heat oil over medium heat and add onion and garlic; sauté for 5 minutes or until soft. Add carrot and red pepper; sauté for 3 minutes. Add barley and cook for 1 minute; stir well. Add water and bouillon cubes, bring to a boil, reduce heat, cover and simmer for 40 minutes or until barley is tender. Season with pepper and serve.

Butter Chicken with Cabbage

Whenever I see a recipe with a variance on Butter Chicken, I immediately want to make it. This one with napa cabbage is a delicious twist. If you plan to make this recipe later in camp, you will need to use freeze-dried chicken and dehydrated yogurt.

1	large onion, finely chopped	1
5	cloves garlic, minced	5
1 cup	sun-dried tomatoes	250 mL
1 cup	water	250 mL
2 tbsp	soft margarine or butter, melted	30 mL
2 tsp	each ground ginger and curry powder	10 mL
1 tsp	each ground cumin, cinnamon and coriander	5 mL
1 lb	▲ chicken thighs, about 6 to 8 pieces	500 g
2 cups	finely shredded Napa cabbage	500 mL
1 tbsp	wine vinegar	15 mL
1 cup	▲ plain yogurt	250 mL

Serves 4

Preparation time:
15 minutes

Cooking time:
1½ minutes

AT HOME: Measure out the ginger, curry powder, cumin, cinnamon and coriander, store in a small container.

AT CAMP: Place the onion, garlic, tomatoes, water, margarine, ginger, curry powder, cumin, cinnamon, coriander and chicken in a Dutch oven (see page 55). Cook chicken for 1½ hours or until chicken will shred easily with a fork. Stir in the Napa cabbage, vinegar and yogurt into chicken, cook for 10 minutes or until hot and the cabbage is wilted.

Country Chili

So very easy, and so very tasty!

Serves 4

Preparation time:
10 minutes

Cooking time:
about 40 minutes

1 lb.	💧 frozen ground beef	500 g
1	large onion, chopped	1
2	garlic cloves, minced	2
½	💧 sweet green pepper, chopped	½
1	can (19 oz/540 mL) beans in tomato sauce	1
1	pkg (7 oz/71g) dried tomato soup mix	1
½ cup	water	125 mL
	chili powder, salt and freshly ground pepper to taste	

AT CAMP: Thaw beef. In a large skillet, cook the beef, onion, garlic and green pepper on medium heat for 5 minutes or until meat is browned and vegetables are tender. Drain off fat, stir in the beans, soup mix, water, chili powder, and salt and pepper to taste. Bring to a boil, reduce heat and simmer for 10 minutes or longer. If mixture is too thick, add a small amount of extra water.

Encore Potatoes

The name of this recipe says it all — everyone always asks for seconds.

Serves 4 to 6

Preparation time:
10 minutes

Cooking time:
35 minutes

4	large cooked baking potatoes	4
1½ cups	sour cream	375 mL
1 cup	grated Cheddar cheese	250 mL
4	green onions, chopped	4
½ tsp	salt and freshly ground pepper	2 mL

AT HOME: In a large saucepan, cook potatoes until fork-tender. When cool enough to handle, grate or finely dice and stir in sour cream, cheese, onions, salt and pepper. Spoon onto a large sheet of foil, seal edges and refrigerate for up to one day, or freeze for longer storage.

AT CAMP: Thaw the sealed potato package, if frozen, then place in a Dutch oven (see page 55). Cook over medium-hot coals for about 30 minutes, or until heated through.

Gin 'n' Tonic Kebabs

The gin in this marinade brings together the flavors of the spices, creating a uniquely delicious dish. We have used it for chicken or pork kebabs. Serve it with our recipe for Quinoa Tabbouleh (page 84) — it is a perfect complement to the kebabs.

Marinade

½ cup	tonic water	125 mL	
½ cup	fresh lime juice	125 mL	
1 tbsp	lime zest	15 mL	
¼ cup	gin	60 mL	
¼ cup	chopped fresh mint or 1 tbsp (15 mL) dried	60 mL	
½ tsp	each ground cinnamon and coriander	2 mL	
2 lbs	frozen boneless chicken breast or pork tenderloin	1 kg	
1	large red onion, peeled and cut into chunks	1	
	wooden or metal skewers		
	salt and freshly ground pepper		

Makes 1 cup (250 mL) marinade

Serves 4 to 5

Preparation time:
15 minutes

Cooking time:
20 minutes

AT HOME: Combine tonic water, lime juice and zest, gin, mint, cinnamon and coriander. Store in a tightly sealed container in the refrigerator, or freeze for longer storage.

AT CAMP: Thaw the gin mixture and the meat, if frozen. Cut meat into 2-inch (5 cm) cubes. Place in a large plastic bag; pour marinade into bag and seal. Allow chicken to marinade no longer than 30 minutes at room temperature, or 1 hour in a cooler. Soak wooden skewers in water for 20 minutes. Remove meat from marinade; discard marinade. Alternately, thread meat cubes and onion on skewers. Season kebabs lightly with salt and pepper, cook over medium-hot coals or on a lightly oiled grill rack for 10 minutes per side, turning once, or until an instant-read thermometer inserted into the center of the chicken reads 165°F (74°C).

Greek-Style Foil-Wrapped Potatoes

These potatoes are a natural accompaniment when serving lamb, even the Stuffed Lamb Burgers (page 144). This easy recipe can be made ahead of time and refrigerated for several hours before grilling.

Serves 4 to 6

Preparation time:
15 minutes

Cooking time:
about 25 minutes

	juice and zest from 1 lemon	
¼ cup	water	60 mL
3 tbsp	olive oil or canola oil	45 mL
2	cloves garlic, minced	2
1 tbsp	chopped fresh rosemary or 1 tsp (5 mL) dried	15 mL
5	medium red or white potatoes, peeled and sliced lengthwise into thick slices	5
¼ cup	crumbled feta cheese	60 mL
	salt, freshly ground pepper	

AT CAMP: In a large plastic bag or bowl, combine the lemon juice and zest, water, oil, garlic and rosemary. Add the potatoes and stir to coat. Spread the potato mixture in one layer, including liquid, on a large sheet of heavy-duty foil. Top with feta cheese and sprinkle lightly with salt and pepper. Fold the edges of foil together to form a tight seal. Place package in a Dutch oven (see page 55) and cook for about 25 minutes over medium-hot coals, or until potatoes are tender and starting to turn golden brown. Open package, sprinkle with extra rosemary and serve.

CAMP TIP: Sliced carrots are a colorful addition to the potatoes and onions.

Grilled Portobello Mushrooms

Early in the trip is the best time to serve these mushrooms along with any grilled meat or the Gin 'n' Tonic Kebabs. They're really easy and they taste great!

4	large portobello mushrooms	4
2 tbsp	each balsamic vinegar and olive oil*	30 mL
1 tsp	each garlic powder and dried basil	5 mL
	salt and freshly ground pepper	

Serves 4

Preparation time:
10 minutes

Cooking time:
about 7 minutes

AT CAMP: Remove stems from mushrooms (see Camp Tip). Place mushrooms in a large re-sealable plastic bag. Pour vinegar, oil, garlic powder and basil over mushrooms; allow to stand for about 30 minutes to marinate. Remove mushrooms from marinade. Grill over an open fire in a wire basket or with a small portable barbecue preheated on medium. If using a grill, remove mushrooms from vinegar mixture; reserve mixture. Place mushrooms on a lightly oiled grill rack. Close lid and cook for 7 minutes or until mushrooms are hot and golden brown; brush occasionally with vinegar mixture. Season to taste with salt and pepper. If open fire cooking, place mushrooms in a grill basket, cook over low embers until mushrooms are golden brown; turn basket frequently for even cooking.

CAMP TIP: Use mushroom stems for soup or to sauté for a pasta sauce.

*You can also use any oil-and-vinegar commercial salad dressing.

Grilled Salmon with Lemon and Herbs

This basic marinade for fish, which can be prepared at home, makes for a perfectly easy camp dinner. You either are a fisherman or not; if not, just bring the salmon from home. Remember: salmon is an excellent source of those essential Omega-3 fatty acids so necessary to keep the body functioning, as our bodies cannot produce them.

Marinade

Serves 4 to 6

Preparation time:
10 minutes

Cooking time:
10 minutes per
1 inch (2.5 cm) thickness

½ cup	fresh lemon juice	125 mL
¼ cup	olive or canola oil	60 mL
1	small onion, finely chopped	1
1	clove garlic, minced	1
2 tbsp	chopped fresh or 2 tsp (10 mL) dried dill	30 mL
4	salmon steaks or fillets	4
	salt and freshly ground pepper	

AT HOME: Combine lemon juice, oil, onion, garlic and dill. Store in a tightly sealed container and refrigerate, or freeze for longer storage.

AT CAMP: Thaw marinade, if frozen. Pour over the salmon, allow to stand for 20 minutes; discard marinade. Place fish skin-side down on a grill rack. Cook over medium-hot coals for 10 minutes per inch (2.5 cm) of thickness, or until fish is opaque and flakes easily with a fork. Season to taste with salt and pepper.

Hawaiian Marinated Pork Chops

So zesty and so easy to prepare, these grilled pork chops are a perfect addition to dinner. If the recipe is used for the first night at camp, marinate the chops in a tightly sealed plastic bag at home. This will allow about 24 hours to marinade to perfection.

Marinade

1 cup	pineapple juice	250 mL	Serves 4
1	small onion, diced	1	**Preparation time:**
1	slice ginger root, diced	1	10 minutes
0 tbsp	soy sauce	15 mL	
2 tbsp	brown sugar	30 mL	**Cooking time:**
1 tbsp	sesame oil	15 mL	6 minutes per side
4	frozen boned pork chops	4	
	salt and freshly ground pepper		

AT HOME: For the marinade, combine pineapple juice, onion, ginger-root, soy sauce, sugar and sesame oil. Add chops to marinade. Store in a tightly sealed plastic bag placed in a cooler or refrigerator.

AT CAMP: Remove chops from marinade; discard marinade. Lightly season chops with salt and pepper, cook over medium-hot coals on a lightly oiled grill rack, turning once, for 5 minutes per side or until an instant-read thermometer inserted into the center of the chops reads 170°F (77°C).

Herb and Garlic Ground Meat Jerky

When making jerky, add enough herbs and spices to bring out the flavor, but be careful not to overwhelm the meat.

Makes 6 oz (175 g)

Preparation time:
15 minutes

Cooking time:
5-6 hours

1 lb	lean ground beef, lamb or pork	500 g
½ cup	chopped onion	125 mL
4–6	cloves garlic	4–6
1 cup	chopped fresh parsley	250 mL
1 tbsp	each: chopped fresh oregano and sage	15 mL
1 tsp	salt	5 mL
½ tsp	freshly ground pepper	2 mL

AT HOME: In food processor, combine meat, onion, garlic, parsley, oregano, sage, salt and pepper. Process until onion, garlic and herbs are finely chopped and mixture has a pastelike consistency.

If you own a piping bag or jerky gun, pipe strips of meat mixture onto parchment-lined baking sheets, leaving about ½ inch (1 cm) between strips. Flatten, if necessary, into ¼ inch (0.5 cm) thickness (see Meat Tip).

Bake in 400°F (200°C) oven for 20 minutes or until meat is well done. Transfer meat to a plate lined with paper towels; blot dry.

Place strips on mesh drying trays. Dry at 155°F (68°C) for 5 to 6 hours or until jerky is firm and flexes and cracks, but does not break. Blot up any excess fat with more paper towels. Allow to cool completely before storing in a tightly sealed container.

MEAT TIP: If you do not own a jerky gun or piping bag, use a rubber spatula and a small spoon to transfer meat mixture into strips on parchment-lined baking sheet. Flatten strips by pressing a second sheet of parchment paper over top of meat. Press down as evenly as possible.

Herb-Stuffed Grilled Fish

Wow — fresh caught and ready to cook! And the pièce de résistance is the fresh lime sauce!

Lime Sauce

	juice and zest from 1 lime	
2 tbsp	olive oil or canola oil	30 mL
1	small clove garlic, crushed	1
2	fresh fish fillets	2
4	fresh dill branches	4
4	stalks fresh chives or green onions	4
	canola oil	
	salt and freshly ground pepper	

Serves 2

Preparation time:
15 minutes

Cooking time:
10 minutes per inch
(2.5 cm) of thickness

AT CAMP: Thaw lime sauce, if frozen. Clean and fillet fish (see page 185). Pat dry with paper towels. Place dill and chives along the length of one fish fillet. Top with second fillet; rub fish lightly with oil. Wrap in foil, secure tightly. Cook over medium-hot coals or on a lightly oiled grill rack for 10 minutes, or until fish is opaque and flakes easily with a fork. Season to taste with salt and pepper. Serve the fish drizzled with Lime Sauce.

Margarita Pizza with Beer Crust

If someone at camp is willing to give up a can of beer, be sure to make this pizza. We love it, and no yeast is needed. And where do some of Margaret's best recipes come from? As she said, there's no gossip, just recipes from her hairdresser friend Darlene. The recipe makes 2 pizza shells; use half of the flour mixture for fewer people.

Crust

Serves 2, 4 or 6

Preparation time:
20 minutes

Cooking time:
20 minutes

3 cups	all-purpose flour	750 mL
1 tbsp	baking powder	15 mL
½ tsp	salt	2 mL
½ tsp	dried oregano or basil	2 mL
1	12 oz (355 mL) can of beer	1

Pizza Filling

	canola or olive oil	
4	medium tomatoes, chopped	4
2 cups	shredded mozzarella cheese	500 mL
¼ cup	grated Parmesan cheese	60 mL
1	large handful chopped fresh basil or 1 tbsp (15 mL) dried	1

AT HOME: Combine flour, baking powder, salt and oregano. Store in a tightly sealed container.

AT CAMP: In a large bowl, combine the flour mixture with beer, stirring slowly just until combined. Turn dough onto a flat, lightly floured surface and knead several times. Pat dough into two pizza pans, being sure to bring dough to the edge of each pan, brush well with oil, top with the chopped tomatoes and basil, sprinkle evenly with the cheeses. Bake in a Dutch oven (see page 55) or on a grill rack on medium heat or Coleman stove. Cut into wedges and serve.

Herb and Garlic Fried Rice

Another one-dish meal, easy and delicious.

3 cups	water	750 mL	Serves 2
¾ cup	long grain white or brown rice	175 mL	
¼ cup	crumbled Herb and Garlic Ground Meat Jerky (page 114)	60 mL	**Preparation time:** 10 minutes
½ cup	sliced carrots	125 mL	
½ cup	chopped broccoli	125 mL	**Cooking time:** 15 minutes
¼ cup	chopped green sweet pepper	60 mL	
1 tbsp	soy sauce	15 mL	

AT CAMP: In large saucepan, bring water to a boil over high heat. Add rice, crumbled jerky, carrots, broccoli and green pepper. Return to boil, reduce heat to medium-low, cover and cook for 15 minutes or until rice is tender and sauce is thickened.

Herb and Garlic Pasta

For a lightweight and high-energy meal, include jerky in this easy pasta sauce recipe.

3 cups	water	750 mL	Serves 2
¼ cup	crumbled Herb and Garlic Ground Meat Jerky (page 114)	60 mL	
¼ cup	dried mushrooms	60 mL	**Preparation time:** 15 minutes
¼ cup	sun-dried tomatoes, chopped	60 mL	
2 cups	dehydrated spaghetti sauce	500 mL	**Cooking time:** 10 minutes
1 cup	broken spaghetti	250 mL	

AT CAMP: In large saucepan, bring water to a boil over high heat. Add crumbled jerky, mushrooms, tomatoes, spaghetti sauce and spaghetti. Return to boil, stirring often. Reduce heat to medium-low, and boil gently for 8 minutes or until pasta is tender and sauce is thickened.

Pan-Fried Potatoes and Mushrooms

These potatoes go with almost any fish or meat. Anytime you are cooking potatoes, double the amount and you'll have a head start on tomorrow's dinner. Any kind of melting cheese will be fine.

Serves 2

Preparation time:
about 10 minutes

Cooking time:
10 minutes

1	small onion, chopped	1
2 tbsp	soft margarine or butter	30 mL
2 cups	diced cooked potatoes	500 mL
½ cup	mushrooms	125 mL
1 cup	grated cheese	250 mL
	salt and freshly ground pepper	

AT CAMP: In a medium skillet, sauté onion in margarine on medium heat for 5 minutes or until tender. Add potatoes and mushrooms; cook for 5 minutes. Add seasonings, sprinkle with cheese, reduce heat, cover and cook for 5 minutes longer, or until cheese is melted. Serve immediately.

Potato Pancakes

Leftover potatoes and eggs are enjoyable served with any grilled meat or chicken.

Serves 2

Preparation time:
5 minutes

Cooking time:
5 minutes

2–3	cooked potatoes, mashed	2–3
2–3	eggs, beaten	2–3
4	green onions, chopped	4
	salt and freshly ground pepper	
	soft margarine or butter	

In a bowl, combine mashed potatoes with beaten eggs, green onions, salt and pepper. Meanwhile, melt margarine in a nonstick skillet; turn potato mixture into skillet, cook on one side until golden brown, flip, cook second side. Serve hot.

Skillet Shrimp and Rice

Consider this recipe a Greek paella — Greek because of the classic shrimp and dill combo, and paella because all ingredients are cooked with rice and served at the table out of the pan. If you can keep feta cheese fresh, this will be a great addition after cooking.

2 tbsp	canola oil or olive oil	30 mL
1	onion, chopped	1
1	sweet yellow or green pepper, cubed	1
1 cup	diced fennel	250 mL
2	cloves garlic, minced	2
1½ cups	long-grain white rice	375 mL
½ cup	white wine	125 mL
2½ cups	chicken broth	625 mL
1 lb	large shrimp, peeled and deveined	500 g
2	tomatoes, seeded and chopped	2
¼ cup	chopped fresh or 1 tbsp (15 mL) dried dill	60 mL
1	lemon, cut into 4 wedges (optional)	1
	salt and freshly ground pepper	

Serves 4

Preparation time:
15 minutes

Cooking time:
about 25 minutes

If using dehydrated vegetables, soak in water for about 30 minutes. In a large nonstick skillet, heat oil over medium heat; cook the onion, sweet pepper, fennel and garlic until tender-crisp, about 5 minutes; stir occasionally. Add rice and cook for 1 minute. Stir in wine until absorbed. Add broth and ½ cup (125 mL) water; bring to a boil. Cover, reduce heat to medium-low and simmer about 12 minutes or until rice is tender but still firm. Stir in the shrimp, tomatoes and dill. Cook, covered, until shrimp are pink (8 to 10 minutes). Add salt and pepper to taste. Serve with lemon wedges, if using.

Slow-Cooked Pulled Pork

Pork, slowly cooked in a tangy sauce until it pulls apart, is delicious. Stir meat shreds into the sauce and serve on onion buns, mashed potatoes or rice.

Sauce

Serves 8

Preparation time:
30 minutes

Cooking time:
4 hours

1 cup	chili sauce	250 mL
⅓ cup	Dijon or grainy mustard	75 mL
⅓ cup	liquid honey	75 mL
2 tbsp	chili powder	30 mL
2 tbsp	◌ tomato paste	30 mL
2 tbsp	Worcestershire sauce	30 mL
1 tbsp	packed brown sugar	15 mL
2 tsp	paprika	10 mL
2	large cloves garlic, minced	2
2 cups	sliced onions	500 mL
3–4 lbs	frozen pork shoulder roast, thawed after roast	1.5–2 kg
2 cups	◌ chopped apples	500 mL
	large ciabatta rolls, onion or crusty buns, mashed potatoes or rice	

AT HOME — SAUCE: Mix together the chili sauce, mustard, honey, chili powder, tomato paste, Worcestershire sauce, brown sugar, paprika and garlic. Store in a tightly sealed container or freeze for longer storage.

AT CAMP: Place onions in the bottom of a Dutch oven (see page 55). Thaw pork, place over onions; top with apples. Pour sauce over meat and apples. Cover and cook on medium heat for 4 hours or until meat is tender and starts to fall apart. Remove meat from oven and place on a large plate. Using 2 forks, shred meat along its length. Stir meat back into sauce.

Tuna Egg Noodle Casserole

This is an all-time favorite using a white milk sauce rather than a high-sodium canned soup. Just add any vegetables the family enjoys. Adding tuna to this recipe is a great way to slip in Omega-3 fatty acids into the diet. Nothing extra is needed other than a salad if you still have napa cabbage in camp.

1½ cups	egg noodles	375 mL	Serves 2
2	3 oz/(85 g each) chunk tuna	2	
½ cup	peas, carrots or mixed vegetables	125 mL	**Preparation time:** 15 minutes
1 tbsp	soft margarine or butter	15 mL	
1 tbsp	whole wheat flour	15 mL	**Cooking time:** 20 minutes
½ cup	milk	125 mL	
⅓ cup	grated mild Cheddar cheese	75 mL	
pinch	freshly ground pepper	pinch	

AT CAMP: In a large saucepan, cook noodles in boiling water according to package directions. Drain well. Combine noodles, tuna and vegetables in a 4 cup (1 L) greased metal pan. In a small saucepan, melt margarine over medium heat. Stir in flour; cook for 2 minutes, stirring constantly, until bubbly. Gradually add milk and cook for 5 minutes or until thickened; stir well. Pour over noodle mixture. Sprinkle with cheese, add pepper, cover with foil and cook in a Dutch oven (see page 55) or near the campfire for about 20 minutes, or until hot and bubbly.

11

Desserts

At times, making dessert may seem too time consuming. It's not. Don't fall into the routine of handing out chocolate bars to everyone to munch on around the campfire. That's not dessert. Besides, desserts can be quite simple to make. Fresh fruit covered in melted chocolate or even caramel pudding served with a shot of Grand Marnier is better than a stale cookie. Just look at the history of the s'more. Since its creation, camping has definitely stepped up a notch.

Apple Cranberry Crisp

This tangy fruit crisp has become a favorite dessert to enjoy at the campsite.

Crisp Topping

Makes 4 to 6 servings

Preparation time:
20 minutes

Cooking time:
about 35 minutes

¼ cup	each: rolled oats, wheat germ and brown sugar	60 mL
¼ cup	soft margarine or butter	60 mL

Fruit Mixture

½ cup	each soft tofu and plain yogurt	125 mL
½ cup	orange juice, divided	125 mL
¼ cup	granulated sugar, divided	60 mL
1 tbsp	whole wheat flour	15 mL
½ tsp	ground cinnamon	2 mL

Fruit

4 cups	sliced, peeled apples (about four medium apples)	1 L
½ cup	cranberries	125 mL

AT HOME: For the topping: Combine rolled oats, wheat germ and brown sugar; cut in margarine until mixture achieves a crumblike consistency. Store in a tightly sealed container and label.

AT CAMP: If using dehydrated tofu and yogurt, rehydrate by adding a small amount of either milk or water, allow to stand about 10 minutes. Stir ¼ cup (60 mL) orange juice concentrate, sugar, tofu, yogurt, flour and cinnamon together. In a medium bowl, combine the apples, cranberries and tofu mixture. Spoon into a 6 cup (1.5 L) greased metal baking pan. Sprinkle evenly with the topping. Place the pan in a Dutch oven (see page 55) and bake at a medium heat for about 35 minutes, or until the apples are tender and the topping is browned.

Banana Brulée

This dessert is deliciously simple to make and even more delicious to eat! If you use this recipe on the first three days out, then you can use fresh bananas; otherwise, use dehydrated bananas. The ricotta mixture, if frozen, will stay fresh for up to three days once it thaws.

1 cup	ricotta cheese (see Camp Tip)	250 mL	Serves 4
¼ cup	lightly packed brown sugar	60 mL	
½ tsp	ground nutmeg	2 mL	**Preparation time:** 15 minutes
1 tsp	vanilla extract	5 mL	
pinch	salt	pinch	**Cooking time:** about 6 minutes
2–3	firm, ripe bananas	2–3	
¼ cup	granulated sugar	60 mL	

AT HOME: In a small bowl, combine ricotta cheese, brown sugar, nutmeg, vanilla and salt. Store in a tightly sealed container and refrigerate, or freeze for longer storage.

AT CAMP: Thaw the ricotta mixture, then spread it in a shallow foil baking dish. Cut the bananas into thin slices and place them around the edge of the foil dish, pressing into the ricotta mixture. Sprinkle with granulated sugar, patting it in an even layer on top of the bananas. Either bake in a Dutch oven (see page 55) or place near the edge of a campfire and bake about 6 minutes, or until the bananas have softened and the sugar has melted, forming a caramelized surface.

CAMP TIP: If you decide to make this recipe at camp, it's a good idea to replace the ricotta cheese with dehydrated 1% cottage cheese. You can replace bananas with fresh or dried mango, pear, or pineapple slices.

Fast 'n' Easy Chocolate Mousse

This silky-smooth treat will truly become tops on the dessert list, especially for chocolate lovers.

Serves 3 to 4

Preparation time:
10 minutes

Cooking time:
about 8 minutes

1 cup	chocolate chips	250 mL
¾ cup	strong coffee	175 mL
¼ cup	milk	60 mL
1 tbsp	rum or brandy	15 mL

AT CAMP: In small saucepan, melt chocolate chips with coffee and milk, heating very slowly, stirring constantly, until chocolate has melted. Stir in rum, spoon mixture into small dishes and cool; if no one wants to wait, just get the spoons ready and dip in.

CAMP TIP: Substitute powdered milk for fresh if you wish to make this later in your trip.

Grilled Fruit Kebabs

This recipe is best enjoyed during the first three days at camp, when the fruits are still fresh. Choose any combination of fresh or canned fruits and grill on individual skewers.

Marinade:

1	large orange	1
¼ cup	granulated sugar	60 mL
2–3 tbsp	dark rum	30–45 mL
½ tsp	ground nutmeg	2 mL

Fruit:

10	pineapple cubes	10
2	bananas, each cut into four pieces	2
2	peaches, peeled and sliced	2
2	plums, halved and pitted	2
2	pears, cut into large pieces	2
	soaked wooden skewers	

Serves 4

Preparation time:
15 minutes

Cooking time:
about 10 minutes

AT HOME: Marinade: Remove zest from orange, squeeze orange for juice. Combine zest, juice, sugar, rum and nutmeg. Store in tightly sealed container and chill or freeze for longer storage.

AT CAMP: If using dehydrated fruits, soak them in water for 30 minutes, then add marinade and soak fruit at room temperature for at least 30 minutes longer. Drain fruit, reserve marinade. Thread fruit alternately on soaked skewers. Preheat grill to medium and spray rack with nonstick coating. Place fruit kebabs on grill rack, grill for 10 minutes or until fruit becomes warm; brush occasionally with the saved marinade; turn kebabs frequently.

Mocha Mousse Cake

This dark chocolate dessert has a mellow flavor and the aroma of rich milk chocolate with a splash of coffee.

Serves 8

Preparation time:
15 minutes

Cooking time:
about 30 minutes

½ cup	unsweetened cocoa powder	125 mL
3 tbsp	all-purpose flour	45 mL
¾ cup	granulated sugar, divided	175 mL
¾ cup	strong coffee	175 mL
½ cup	semisweet or bittersweet chocolate chips	125 mL
1 tsp	vanilla extract	5 mL
2	eggs	2

At home or at camp:

Line 8 inch (20 cm) foil baking pan with parchment paper; lightly oil sides of pan.

In heavy saucepan, combine cocoa, flour and half the sugar. Stir in enough coffee to form a smooth paste. Mix in remaining coffee, cook over medium heat, stirring constantly, until mixture begins to thicken. Simmer for 2 minutes. Immediately stir in chocolate chips, stirring until chocolate has melted and is very smooth. Stir in vanilla.

With wire whisk, beat eggs with remaining sugar for about 5 minutes or until volume has doubled and eggs are very light and fluffy. One-third at a time, fold eggs into chocolate mixture. Pour batter into prepared pan, set pan in Dutch Oven (see page 55) and add boiling water to halfway up sides of baking pan.

Bake for 30 minutes or until cake has risen and the surface springs back when lightly touched. The cake will still jiggle in the center and the interior will be quite gooey. Remove pan from hot water and cool.

To unmold cake, slide a thin knife around sides of cake then invert onto a plate. Remove paper and when you can no longer wait, dig in and enjoy.

MORE S'MORES

S'mores have been a camp tradition ever since the recipe first appeared in the 1927 edition of the Girl Scout handbook. And there's no doubt why it was given its name — short for "some more."

To date no one seems to know who actually started toasting a marshmallow over a campfire. It was probably some camp counselor who couldn't stand baking up another can of pork and beans. But it's in the United States where most are now consumed — 90 million pounds (over 40 million kg) per year to be exact. The majority of those consumers are, no surprise, under the age of 12. Truth is, parents loathe the making of s'mores on camping trips. The gooey mess gets all over the kids' clothes, making them bear bait for the rest of the evening. So try these not-so-sticky recipes.

S'MORE CREPES

S'mores are pretty much downgraded versions of a fancy French crepe. Spread chocolate-hazelnut spread on a soft tortilla, sprinkle icing sugar and coconut shavings on top, roll up in a piece of foil and roast in the campfire or a Dutch oven.

MEXICAN S'MORES

Spread a generous amount of peanut butter on a soft tortilla, add a layer of chocolate chips and mini marshmallows and then roll up the tortilla. Wrap it in foil and cook over a fire on a grill for just under five minutes. Unwrap and eat with a spoon.

SQUIRTY S'MORES

Toast a marshmallow over the fire and then, without removing it from the stick, roll it in a pie plate a quarter full of Hershey's chocolate syrup and crushed graham crackers.

Mixed Drinks

Serving a couple of cocktails, a mug of wine, a dram of single malt or a splash of Irish cream in the morning coffees can really add to good group dynamics on any type of camping trip.

After a long day, there's no better way to wind down than to sip elegantly on what is commonly known by all "happy campers" as the Bush Martini.

Beginners usually go for the simple but effective pouring of equal parts gin and cherry-flavored drink crystals in an enamel coffee cup — served shaken, not stirred, in a Nalgene water bottle. But its presentation is less than civilized.

There's the classic Cosmopolitan: 4 parts vodka, 2 parts triple sec, 2 parts cranberry juice crystals mixed with water and a squirt of lime juice. It's a tad boring though.

The ultimate, however, is what's called the Blue Sky: 1 ounce (30 mL) vodka, ¼ ounce (7 mL) sweet vermouth, ¼ ounce (7 mL) Blue Curacao and, to finish, garnish with three plump blueberries skewered on a long dried up pine needle. Now that's the perfect Bush Martini.

When it comes to cocktails, the camping culture is very experimental. Here are a few favorites.

Swamp Water

The name comes from what it looks like after it's mixed up — swamp water.

1 ounce (30 mL) vodka
1 splash Blue Curacao
1 package orange drink crystals and water sufficient to mix

Mix up the orange drink in a Nalgene bottle. Pour the vodka and Blue Curacao into a cup and then add drink mix to taste.

Hurricane

This is a darn good drink to have while you're huddled under the rain tarp.

1 ounce (30 mL) dark rum
1 splash grenadine
4 ounces (120 mL) grapefruit juice crystals mixed with water
2 ounces (60 mL) orange/mango drink crystals mixed with water

Mix everything except the grenadine in a container, and then add grenadine until the drink turns red.

Algonquin Martini

This is a good recipe simply because of the name. Algonquin is a well-known canoe park in Ontario, Canada.

1½ ounces (45 mL) Canadian Club whiskey or other Canadian or rye whiskey
1 ounce (30 mL) dry vermouth
1 ounce (30 mL) pineapple juice
1 ounce (30 mL) club soda

Blend the whiskey, vermouth and juice together in a mixing container. Shake. Pour into a mug and top off with club soda.

Cinnamon Stick Martini

Make sure to include the cinnamon stick and garnish!

2 ounces (60 mL) gold (or amber) rum
1 ounce (30 mL) applejack
1 teaspoon (5 mL) ground cinnamon
1 cinnamon stick
1 apple slice, for garnish

Mix the rum, applejack and cinnamon together in a mixing container; then pour into a mug, stir with the cinnamon stick and add the apple slice for garnish.

Mexican Coffee

This "spirited" coffee will definitely lift up your spirits.

¼ cup (60 mL) powdered cocoa
¾ cup (175 mL) packed brown sugar
2 teaspoons (10 mL) ground cinnamon
5 cups (1.25 L) strong coffee
Kahlua or Tia Maria
Whipped cream or canned milk

In a large pan, combine cocoa, sugar, cinnamon and coffee. Bring to a gentle simmer, stirring well until sugar dissolves and coffee is hot. Pour into mugs, add liqueur and if available whipped cream (or canned milk when whipped cream is gone).

Irish Coffee

An Irish chef created this recipe for passengers who had made an emergency landing at an Irish airport. Serves 2. Prep. time: 5 min.

½ cup (125 mL) chilled whipping cream or canned milk
1 tablespoon (15 mL) granulated sugar
3 oz (90 mL) Irish whiskey, divided
Hot strong coffee

In a small bowl, whip cream with sugar until stiff peaks form, or stir sugar into canned milk. Divide whiskey between 2 large coffee mugs. Fill three-quarters full with hot coffee, top with whipped cream, or stir in sweetened canned milk.

Wake Up and Smell the Coffee Martini

This is a great recipe to have on a cold afternoon. Just make sure to measure the ingredients as precisely as you can to get the best flavor.

2 ounces (60 mL) vodka
1 ounce (30 mL) dry vermouth
1 ounce (30 mL) hazelnut liqueur (such as Frangelico)
6 coffee beans

Pour all of the spirits into a mixing container, shake and then pour into a mug. Add the coffee beans for garnish.

Rob Roy Martini

John MacGregor's book *A Thousand Miles in the Rob Roy Canoe* spawned a huge interest in recreational canoeing.

3 ounces (90 mL) scotch
½ teaspoon (2 mL) dry vermouth
1 lemon twist, for garnish

Pour all of the spirits into a mixing container, shake and then pour into a mug. Add the garnish.

Tea Time Martini

The key ingredient in the conception of this recipe was a bag of chamomile tea that no one had bothered brewing.

2 ounces (60 mL) vodka
½ cup (125 mL) chamomile tea
1 tablespoon (15 mL) lemon juice
1 lemon wedge, for garnish

Pour the vodka, tea and lemon juice into a mixing container, shake and then pour into a mug. Add the garnish.

Wine

Not only does sipping wine add to a trip, using it for cooking greatly enhances the flavor of your meals and turns what could be a drab moment in camp life into a cultural experience. There's no better way to impress your camping companions than to add a dash of red wine to reconstituted spaghetti sauce or white wine to a white sauce that's then poured over baked fish fillets. In fact, any meal that requires water can be greatly enhanced by replacing about half the liquid with wine.

Top-Rated Boxed Wines

Whites

Banrock Station Unwooded Chardonnay (Australia): Crisp and fruity, this wine has citrus and stone-fruit flavors.

Three Thieves "Bandit" Pinot Grigio (California): Light, crisp, and simple.

Reds

Banrock Station Shiraz (Australia): Classic berry fruit and black pepper.

Red Lips Syrah (France): Juicy and ripe with flavors of blackberry, cherry, plum, vanilla and a surprising hit of tannin.

Le Petit Sommelier Shiraz/Grenache (France): The peppery spice of Shiraz with the fresh, juicy berry flavor of Grenache.

Sober Sangria

Anyone who does not like their Sangria made with wine, will go nuts when offered this version! Makes 8 cups (2 L). Prep. time: 5 min.

1 can (6 oz/170 mL) frozen orange juice concentrate
1 cup (250 mL) cranberry juice
2 tablespoons (30 mL) fresh lemon juice
½ cup (125 mL) diced fruit
3 cups (750 mL) club soda

Combine orange, cranberry and lemon juice in large container. Keep cool and just before serving add the soda water.

Hot Toddies

Drinking a hot toddy may not be as innocent as sipping plain hot chocolate, but it's far less harsh than gulping down shots of scotch. It's also less potent than a martini but seems just as civilized. And they're darn good to savor around the campfire if you want the night to seem less chilled, the stars somewhat brighter and friends more pleasant to be with. The alcohol used in a hot toddy is traditionally brandy, rum or whiskey. To that you can add either tea, coffee or hot chocolate. Sweeteners such as honey, sugar or syrup are then added.

African Delight

1 ounce (30 mL) brandy
1 tablespoon (15 mL) honey
1 cup (250 mL) hot water
1 bag Rooibos herbal tea
¼ lemon

Coat the bottom of a camp mug with honey then add the brandy and the juice from the lemon slice. Boil water and steep the tea bag for 5–7 minutes. Pour the hot tea into the mug.

Chocolate Buzz

1 ounce (30 mL) Irish cream
½ cup (125 mL) instant espresso powder
¾ cup (175 mL) hot water
½ teaspoon (2 mL) ground cinnamon
1 chunk semisweet chocolate

Pour the boiled water into a camp mug and add the espresso, Irish cream and ground cinnamon. Grate the chunk of chocolate and sprinkle on top.

Irish (True Grit) Coffee

True camp coffee is nothing but real grounds and water in the pot coffee. Bring water to a rolling boil, take it off the heat source, dump in 1 generous tablespoon (15 mL) coffee grounds per 1 cup (250 mL) water and let it steep (covered) alongside the campfire for approximately five to 10 minutes.

The most crucial element of brewing "true grit" is to never let the coffee boil once you've taken it off the heat source. The reason for the bad taste of boiled coffee is the bitter tannins and flavoring oils it contains. The tasty oils are released at 205°F (96°C), just below boiling point. The bitter acids, however, are released right at or just above the boiling point.

Another important factor is how to settle the grounds before serving the coffee. Some campers throw pieces of eggshell in or toss in a few round pebbles. A teaspoon of cold water seems to do the trick as well, or simply tapping the side of the pot three or four times with a knife or spoon.

Sun Tea

When time permits, never will you taste a better cup of iced tea than that made in the sun.

To make sun tea: If you have a large container, preferably glass or clear plastic will do, place 2 tea bags for every 4 cups (1 L) of cold water in the container, cover and let stand in the hot sun for 3–4 hours. If the sun is not intense, increase the time accordingly. Remove tea bags, squeezing gently. To serve, pour tea over ice cubes, if available, or just try to find cool water to immerse the container. A lemon wedge is nice, but tea is so very refreshing that it may not even need to be sweetened or treated with lemon.

Weekend Gourmet

Due to the need to keep foods cold, a number of our recipes were not suitable for longer camping trips. Thus we decided to include them in this chapter called "Weekend Gourmet." Many boaters, sail as well as power, use their boats as a cottage each weekend. Some campers are weekend warriors too. Naturally the recipes in this chapter are taking advantage of being away for a shorter length of time, and the ice will not thaw over a two- to three-day weekend — a true advantage when planning menus and recipes that need to be kept chilled. Many campers can only manage to get away for these short trips. Bon appétit!

Avocado Pesto Dip

After a tiring day of hiking, several canoe portages, or a windy day on the water, this dip will satisfy as a fast pickup snack loaded with calories when served with nacho or corn chips. Try tossing it into cooked pasta, or use as a topping with freshly caught fish. You decide — bring all the ingredients with you or make it at home and freeze it.

Makes ¾ cup (175 mL)

Preparation time:
about 10 minutes

¼ cup	pine nuts, toasted	60 mL
1 cup	coarsely mashed avocado (1 large)	250 mL
2 tbsp	finely grated Parmesan cheese	30 mL
1 tbsp	minced fresh cilantro or parsley	15 mL
1–2 tbsp	fresh lime juice	15–30 mL
2 tbsp	olive oil	30 mL
	salt and freshly ground pepper	
	raw vegetables, crackers, and nacho or corn chips	

AT HOME: In a food processor, blend pine nuts until coarsely chopped. Add avocado, cheese, cilantro and lime juice; blend until smooth. Gradually add oil and season to taste with salt and pepper. Store in a tightly sealed container in the refrigerator, or freeze for longer storage.

AT CAMP: Allow dip to thaw and serve with crackers, raw vegetables or chips.

Baked Vegetable Loaf

Many vegetables in combination with rolled oats add a fabulous extra flavor to this nonmeat loaf. It's as easy as making meatloaf in your home oven, but with much more flavor due to the smoking that occurs during grilling.

2 tbsp	canola oil	30 mL	
1½ cups	peeled diced sweet potato	375 mL	
1½ cups	cubed zucchini	375 mL	
1½ cups	cubed sweet red pepper	375 mL	
½	small red onion, chopped	½	
½ cup	chicken broth	125 mL	
⅔ cup	rolled oats	150 mL	
1	egg, lightly beaten	1	
2 tbsp	chopped fresh or 1 tbsp (15 mL) dried oregano	30 mL	

Serves 4

Preparation time:
20 minutes

Cooking time:
40 minutes

AT CAMP: In a nonstick skillet, heat oil on medium high; cook sweet potato for 5 minutes or until light brown and almost tender. Add zucchini, red pepper and onion; cook for 3 minutes or until pepper and onion are softened. Add broth, reduce heat, cover and cook for 5 minutes or until vegetables are tender: remove cover and simmer until liquid is reduced. Cool mixture before combining with rolled oats, egg and oregano; stir gently just until mixed. Turn mixture into a greased metal loaf pan. Cover and place in a cooler for 1 hour to firm up loaf. Place loaf pan on a camp stove in a large skillet. Add a small amount of water to skillet. Cover and cook on medium-high heat for 40 minutes or until loaf is firm and will hold together. Remove loaf from skillet, cover with foil and let rest for about 10 minutes before slicing.

Cappuccino Crème

This light and very flavorful dessert, which we suggest you accompany with a few fresh berries or other fruit, will make a festive finish for a camp meal. Keep the dessert chilled in the cooler, as it is perfect for that gourmet weekend.

Serves 4

Preparation time:
10 minutes

Cooking time:
3 hours

1	envelope plain gelatin	1
½ cup	cold water	125 mL
1½ cups	very strong coffee	375 mL
1 cup	whipping cream, whipped	250 mL
	chocolate curls	

AT HOME: Soften the gelatin in water for 5 minutes. Add to hot coffee; stir until gelatin is dissolved. Chill and, when mixture is cold, fold in whipped cream. Spoon into a large container; cover and chill until set. Top with chocolate curls and enjoy after your first dinner at camp.

Carrot Crisp

Serves 4 to 6

Preparation time:
15 minutes

Cooking time:
30 minutes

4 cups	chopped carrots	1 L
1 tbsp	soft margarine or butter	15 mL
½ tsp	ground ginger	2 mL

Topping

¼ cup	toasted sunflower seeds	60 mL
¼ cup	toasted ground almonds	60 mL
¼ cup	crumbs, whole wheat bread or cracker	60 mL
2 tbsp	sesame seeds	30 mL
2 tbsp	soft margarine or butter, melted	30 mL
	salt and freshly ground pepper	

AT HOME OR AT CAMP: In a large saucepan, cook carrots in boiling water for 10 minutes or until tender. Drain and mash; stir in margarine and ginger. Spoon into a lightly greased metal baking pan. Topping: Combine sunflower seeds, almonds, bread crumbs, sesame seeds and melted margarine; add salt and pepper to taste. Spoon over carrots, bake in a Dutch oven (see page 55) for 30 minutes or until heated, or set close to open fire to heat slowly.

Camping Burgers

More than likely you will choose one of these burgers per camping trip, due to the need to keep frozen, then cook them after thawing. Game Burgers will be the leanest of the meat burgers, and will thus require more care in cooking. Cook all ground beef until well-done, 160°F (70°C) in the center.

AT CAMP: For all burger recipes, thaw patties. Cook over medium-hot coals or on a lightly oiled grill rack for 5 minutes per side, or until an instant-read thermometer inserted into the center of each patty reads 160°F (71°C). Warm and fill each bun with a cooked patty and toppings of your choice.

CAMP TIP: Since Game Burgers are very lean, take care not to overcook them, but keep in mind that all ground meats should be cooked to well-done.

Game Burgers

1 lb	ground venison, bison or elk	500 g	
½ cup	rolled oats	125 mL	
⅓ cup	salsa or chili sauce	75 mL	
1	egg, beaten	1	
pinch	salt and freshly ground pepper	pinch	
4 to 6	crusty buns, halved	4 to 6	
	mustard, chili sauce, relish		

Makes 4 to 6 patties

Preparation time:
10 minutes

Cooking time:
5 minutes per side

AT HOME: In a bowl, combine meat, rolled oats, salsa, egg, salt and pepper. If salsa is runny, you may need extra oats to hold patties together. Gently form into four to six evenly shaped patties. Wrap each patty in plastic wrap or foil to keep separated. Refrigerate or freeze until ready to use.

Stuffed Lamb Burgers

Makes 4 double patties

Preparation time:
10 minutes

Cooking time:
6 minutes per side

1 lb.	lean ground lamb	500 g
⅓ cup	dried bread crumbs	75 mL
2 tbsp	chopped fresh mint or 1 tsp (5 mL) dried	30 mL
2	small cloves garlic, chopped	2
½ tsp	each salt and ground cinnamon	2 mL
pinch	freshly ground pepper and hot pepper flakes	pinch
½ cup	crumbled feta cheese	125 mL
4	pita breads, halved	4

AT HOME: In a medium bowl, combine the lamb, bread crumbs, mint, garlic, salt, cinnamon, pepper and pepper flakes. Gently form into eight thin, evenly shaped patties. Divide feta cheese over four patties. Place the remaining patties over cheese and press to seal edges. Wrap each patty in plastic wrap or foil to keep separated. Refrigerate or freeze until ready to use.

Chicken or Turkey Burgers

Makes 4 patties

Preparation time:
10 minutes

Cooking time:
6 minutes per side

Panko crumbs can be a replacement for regular dried bread crumbs. They are a Japanese-style bread crumb and are excellent for helping to shape and hold patties together.

1 lb.	lean ground chicken or turkey	500 g
⅓ cup	Panko crumbs or dried bread crumbs	75 mL
1	egg, beaten	1
¼ cup	sour cream or plain yogurt	60 mL
2	green onions, chopped	2
1 tsp	each dried thyme and oregano	5 mL
½ tsp	each salt and freshly ground pepper	2 mL
4	whole wheat buns, halved	4

AT HOME: In a bowl, combine chicken, crumbs, egg, sour cream, onions, thyme, oregano, salt and pepper. Gently form into four evenly shaped patties. Wrap each patty in plastic wrap or foil to keep separated. Refrigerate or freeze until ready to use.

Beef Burgers

1 lb.	ground beef	500 g	Makes 4 patties
1	small onion, finely chopped	1	
1	clove garlic, minced	1	**Preparation time:**
1	egg, beaten	1	10 minutes
⅓ cup	rolled oats	75 mL	**Cooking time:**
2 tbsp	ketchup or chili sauce	30 mL	6 minutes per side
½ tsp	salt and freshly ground pepper	2 mL	
4	cheese or onion buns, halved	4	

AT HOME. In a bowl, combine the beef, onion, garlic, egg, rolled oats, ketchup, salt and pepper. Gently form into four evenly shaped patties. Wrap each patty in plastic wrap or foil to keep separated. Refrigerate or freeze until ready to use.

Bulgur Black Bean Burgers

This vegetarian-style burger will satisfy all tastes, whether you are vegetarian or not. It's also a good way to meet protein requirements

1 cup	water	250 mL	Makes 4 burgers
½ cup	bulgur	125 mL	
1	can (19 oz./598 mL) black beans	1	**Preparation time:**
2 tbsp	plain yogurt	30 mL	15 minutes
½ tsp	each ground allspice, cinnamon, cumin	2 mL	**Cooking time:**
4	whole wheat buns, halved	4	8 minutes
	sliced tomato and shredded lettuce		

AT HOME: In a small saucepan, bring water to a boil; add bulgur, cover and cook for 10 minutes or until water is absorbed and bulgur is tender. Set aside. Drain bulgur and rinse beans. In a bowl, mash beans with yogurt until almost smooth. Stir in bulgur, allspice, cinnamon and cumin. Shape into four burger-size patties. Wrap each patty in plastic wrap or foil to keep separated. Refrigerate or freeze until ready to use.

Caramelized Onions

All of the above burgers will benefit when topped with a dollop of Caramelized Onions. A small splash of balsamic vinegar or wine to de-glaze the pan after cooking gives extra oomph. This is a great topping for baked or mashed potatoes, any burger, scrambled eggs, grilled vegetables, fish, steak, pork chops. We add them to other cooked vegetables for extra flavor.

Makes 2 cups (500 mL)

Preparation time:
10 minutes

Cooking time:
45 minutes

5	large onions	5
	olive oil and soft margarine or butter	
	salt and granulated sugar (optional)	

AT HOME: Slice off the root and top ends of onions and peel. Cut onions in half, then place cut-side down and slice lengthwise from top to bottom in desired thickness. Cover bottom of a wide, heavy pan with oil or a mixture of oil and margarine, about 1 tsp (5 mL) per onion. Heat the pan on medium-high heat until oil shimmers. Add onions and stir to coat, spreading slices over pan. Cook, stirring occasionally, on medium for 10 minutes, then sprinkle with salt and sugar if using. Continue cooking, still stirring, until onions are caramelized, about 30 more minutes.

If onion mixture starts to become too dry, add a small amount of water and keep cooking. Leave onions alone during cooking; if you stir them too much they will not brown. Let them start to stick to bottom of pan, as you can always add water to keep moist. As onions cook down you may lower the cooking heat. Stay in the vicinity of the stove while caramelizing.

Caramelized Onion Dip

Add ⅓ cup (75 mL) Caramelized Onions to 1 cup (250 mL) sour cream or plain yogurt; taste and add more onions if needed. This may easily be the best onion dip ever!

Crustless Vegetable Cottage Cheese Quiche

Similar to a quiche, this pie uses cottage cheese along with eggs for extra protein and calcium. Adding some vegetables provides great color, as well as extra fiber.

4	eggs, lightly beaten	4
1	container (16 oz/500 g) cottage cheese	1
½ cup	plain yogurt	125 mL
¼ cup	whole wheat flour	60 mL
¼ tsp	each salt and freshly ground pepper	1 mL
1 cup	fresh whole wheat bread crumbs	250 mL
1 cup	finely chopped mixed vegetables (carrot, zucchini, onion and mushroom)	250 mL
½ cup	water	125 mL

Serves 4

Preparation time:
20 minutes

Cooking time:
35 minutes

AT CAMP: In a large bowl, combine eggs, cottage cheese, yogurt, flour, salt and pepper. Stir ⅓ cup (75 mL) egg mixture into bread crumbs; press into a 9 inch (23 cm) greased metal pie plate. Stir mixed vegetables and ½ cup (125 mL) water into remaining egg mixture; spoon over bread crumbs. Place pie plate in a Dutch oven (see page 55). Bake for 25 minutes or until quiche is puffy and set in the center — it will start to send out a cooked aroma. Remove from oven and let stand for 10 minutes before cutting into wedges.

Goat Cheese Bruschetta

How wonderful these small bites taste when heated over an open fire! Bruschetta is the original Italian garlic bread, a rustic version brushed with olive oil and toasted over coals — its name means "roast over coals." Today it typically means grilled slices of crusty bread topped with whatever you choose; chopped tomatoes, a variety of cheeses, garlic, caramelized onions — the options are numerous. Buon appetito! Bruschetta and a glass of red wine will improve the world!

Serves 3 to 4

Preparation time:
10 minutes

Cooking time:
2 to 3 minutes

1	small onion, thinly sliced	1
2 tbsp	olive oil	30 mL
1	clove garlic, minced	1
2	small coarsely chopped tomatoes	2
1	log (4 oz/113 g) goat cheese, crumbled	1
12	thick slices bread	12
	salt and freshly ground pepper to taste	

AT CAMP: In a small skillet over medium heat, sauté onion in hot oil for 5 minutes or until onion is tender. Add garlic, cook for 30 seconds longer. Remove from heat. Combine tomatoes, cheese, salt and pepper with cooked onions. Grill bread until toasted, brushing with more olive oil. Top each slice of bread with tomato-cheese mixture.

Granola Brunch Bread

For double the use and enjoyment of the recipe in the Breakfasts chapter for Family-Style Granola (page 69), we really encourage you to make this bread. It's easy to bake at camp in a Dutch oven or on a boat or camper trailer where you may have a built-in oven.

1¾ cups	all-purpose flour	425 mL	Serves 3
1 tsp	each baking powder and baking soda	5 mL	
½ tsp	each ground nutmeg and cinnamon	2 mL	**Preparation time:** 15 minutes
pinch	salt	pinch	
1 cup	plain yogurt	250 mL	**Cooking time:**
1	egg	1	35 minutes
2 tsp	vanilla extract	10 mL	
1 cup	granulated sugar	250 mL	
¼ cup	soft margarine or butter	60 mL	
⅔ cup	Family-Style Granola	150 mL	

AT HOME: In a large bowl, combine flour, baking powder, baking soda, nutmeg, cinnamon and salt. Store in a tightly sealed container. In a small bowl, combine yogurt, egg and vanilla. Refrigerate in a tightly sealed container until needed.

AT CAMP: In a large bowl, cream the sugar with margarine; add yogurt mixture and stir until creamy. Stir in dry ingredients and spoon into a greased 8-inch (2 L) metal baking pan. Sprinkle with granola. Place pan in a Dutch oven (see page 55). Bake for 35 minutes or until cake springs back when lightly touched. Cool on a wire rack until your hunger pangs can't let you wait any longer.

Grilled Banana Oatmeal Pancakes

Here is a perfect recipe for a camp breakfast or as an after-dinner dessert. Either bring everything pre-measured from home or make from scratch at camp. Fire up the grill or camp stove and start the pancakes by stirring liquid ingredients into dry ingredients and get cooking.

Makes: 14 pancakes

Preparation time:
10 minutes

Cooking time:
about 5 minutes per batch

1 cup	large-flake rolled oats	250 mL
1 cup	whole wheat flour	250 mL
¼ cup	lightly packed brown sugar	60 mL
1 tsp	each baking powder and baking soda	5 mL
¼ tsp	each salt and ground cinnamon	1 mL
1	ripe banana, mashed	1
2	eggs, beaten	2
1 cup	plain yogurt	250 mL
½ cup	milk	125 mL
¼ cup	canola oil	60 mL
1 tsp	vanilla extract	5 mL
	nonstick cooking spray or oil	

AT HOME: In a large bowl, combine rolled oats, flour, sugar, baking powder, baking soda, salt and cinnamon. Store in a tightly sealed container. In a small bowl, combine mashed banana, eggs, yogurt, milk, oil and vanilla. Store in a tightly sealed container and refrigerate or freeze for longer storage.

AT CAMP: Stir banana mixture into dry ingredients just until blended. Heat a large nonstick skillet over medium heat (a drop of water will sizzle). Spray with nonstick cooking spray or add some oil. Drop batter by the large spoonfuls onto pan. Cook pancakes for 3 minutes or until bubbles break on the surface and the underside is golden brown; turn and cook second side until golden.

Lamb Chops with Rosemary and Grapes

Grapes provide a fruity sauce with the addition of a touch of honey, wine and rosemary.

1 tbsp	canola oil	15 mL	Serves 4
8	loin lamb chops, about 1¼ inch (3 cm) thick	8	**Preparation time:**
	salt and freshly ground black pepper		15 minutes
3 tbsp	chopped fresh rosemary, divided	45 mL	
4	cloves garlic, minced	4	**Cooking time:**
2 cups	red grapes	500 mL	about 15 minutes
⅓ cup	dry white wine	75 mL	
1 tsp	liquid honey	5 mL	

AT CAMP: In a large skillet, heat oil over medium-high heat (a drop of water will sizzle). Place chops in pan; season lightly with salt and pepper. Sprinkle chops with half of the rosemary in the spaces between chops. Cook for 5 minutes, then turn and sprinkle with garlic; cook for 3 minutes longer for medium-rare, or longer to suit your taste. Remove chops from pan; keep warm while making sauce.

Pour off most of the fat from the skillet. Add grapes and remaining rosemary, then reduce heat and cook, stirring frequently, for 5 minutes or until grapes soften. Stir in wine and honey, simmer for 2 minutes, pour over chops and serve.

Marinade for the Fresh Catch

Fish cooked on the grill couldn't be easier or more delicious when you use the right technique. If you have a lucky catch of fresh, fabulous fish for dinner, you could simply throw it right into a pan, but if you're in a more adventurous mood, you might like to bring this marinade from home. Fish cooks quickly, so be careful not to overcook it.

Marinade

Serves 2 to 4

Preparation time:
10 minutes

Cooking time:
10 minutes per inch
(2.5 cm) thickness

¼ cup	dry white wine	60 mL
1 tbsp	Dijon mustard	15 mL
1 tbsp	horseradish	15 mL
1 tbsp	Thai or Asian chili sauce	15 mL
1 tbsp	soy sauce	15 mL
1 tbsp	sesame oil	15 mL
2	fish fillets (about ½ lb/250 g each)	2
	sliced lemon	

AT HOME: In a small bowl, combine wine, mustard, horseradish, chili sauce, soy sauce and sesame oil and store in a tightly sealed container.

AT CAMP: In a shallow pan, arrange fish fillets. Pour marinade over fish and turn fish to coat. Allow fish to marinate in a cooler or refrigerator for several hours. Drain marinade and discard. Place fish in aluminum foil, top with lemon slices and secure foil tightly. Cook in a covered skillet on a camp stove or in coals of a camp fire for 10 minutes or until fish is opaque and flakes easily with a fork.

Raisin French Toast with Spiced Orange Maple Blueberry Sauce

French toast is a hit with all ages. Other berries, such as raspberries or strawberries, may replace the blueberries.

Sauce

Makes 2 cups (500 mL)

2 cups	fresh or frozen blueberries	500 mL
¼ cup	fresh orange juice	60 mL
1 tsp	grated orange zest	5 mL
1	cinnamon stick	1
1	small piece candied ginger, diced	1
½ cup	each granulated sugar and maple syrup	125 mL

French Toast

4	eggs	4
½ cup	milk	125 mL
1 tsp	ground cinnamon	5 mL
10	slices raisin bread	10
	nonstick cooking spray or oil	

Serves 4

Preparation time:
10 minutes

Cooking time:
10 minutes

AT CAMP. SAUCE: In a medium pan, combine blueberries, orange juice and zest, cinnamon stick and ginger. Bring to a boil over high heat; reduce heat and simmer for 5 minutes. Stir in the sugar and syrup; continue cooking until sugar has dissolved. Remove from heat and cool. Discard cinnamon stick and store in a tightly sealed container and refrigerate or freeze for longer storage.

FRENCH TOAST: In a shallow dish, combine eggs, milk and cinnamon. Dip each bread slice into egg mixture. Turn to coat, soaking up egg mixture. Spray a skillet with nonstick cooking spray, add bread and cook over medium heat for 2 minutes. Turn and cook second side for 2 minutes or until golden brown. Serve with warm sauce.

Salmon, Shrimp and Vegetable Kebabs

A hint of Asian flavors in the sherry marinade dresses up this recipe for grilled salmon, shrimp and vegetables.

Serves 2

Preparation time:
15 minutes

Cooking time:
about 10 minutes

Sherry Marinade

2 tbsp	dry sherry	30 mL
2 tsp	each sesame oil and soy sauce	10 mL
1 tsp	grated gingerroot	5 mL
1	clove garlic, minced	1

Seafood and Vegetables

8	jumbo shrimp	8
1	thick salmon fillet (¼ lb/125 g)	1
4	cubes each sweet red and green pepper	4
6	medium mushrooms	6
2	metal or soaked wooden skewers	2

AT HOME. MARINADE: Combine sherry, sesame oil, soy sauce, gingerroot and garlic; store in a tightly sealed container.

AT CAMP: Clean shrimp and cube salmon; marinate in sherry marinade for up to 2 hours. Blanch pepper cubes in a small amount of boiling water for 1 minute; drain well. Remove seafood from marinade. In a small saucepan, bring marinade to a boil; simmer for 5 minutes and keep warm. Thread shrimp, salmon and vegetables alternately on 2 skewers. Preheat a grill or large nonstick skillet on medium-high heat. Place kebabs on an oiled grill rack or in a skillet; cook for 10 minutes or until salmon and shrimp are opaque; turn once or twice, basting occasionally with warm marinade.

Slow-Roasted Fresh Fish with Pea Purée

Pea purée is a colorful focus to set off the wonderful flavors of fresh-caught fish.

Pea Purée

2 cups	frozen peas, thawed	500 mL
½ cup	fresh mint leaves	125 mL
2	cloves garlic, minced	2
¼ cup	canola oil or olive oil	60 mL
¼ cup	grated Parmesan cheese	00 mL
	salt and freshly ground pepper, to taste	
	lemon wedges	

Fish

2 tbsp	canola oil or olive oil	30 mL
1	lemon	1
2	fillets salmon or fresh-caught fish	2
	salt and freshly ground pepper to taste	

AT HOME. PEA PURÉE: In a food processor, process peas, mint and garlic until coarsely chopped. Slowly add oil and cheese; process until smooth. Season to taste with salt and pepper. Store purée in a tightly sealed container and refrigerate until needed.

AT CAMP: Place oil in a small bowl. Zest the lemon, add to oil. Brush evenly over fish and let stand for 20 minutes to infuse flavor into fish. Sprinkle lightly with salt and pepper. Bake covered in a 250°F (120°C) oven or Dutch oven (see page 55) for 25 minutes, or until fish flakes easily with two forks. Serve a spoonful of pea purée on each plate, and top with fish and a lemon wedge.

Steak Sauce

We are delighted with this sauce, as most others are far too salty. It keeps very well without refrigeration. The name says it all — we use it for steaks, but one day we tried it with pork chops and it was equally good.

Makes 1 cup (250 mL)

Preparation time:
5 minutes

Cooking time:
2 minutes

½ cup	balsamic vinegar	125 mL
2	small cloves garlic, crushed	2
¼ cup	malt vinegar	60 mL
2 tbsp	Worcestershire sauce	30 mL
2 tbsp	tomato paste	30 mL
2 tsp	brown sugar	10 mL
pinch	salt and freshly ground pepper	pinch

AT HOME OR AT CAMP: In a small saucepan, cook balsamic vinegar and garlic for 2 minutes, or until reduced by half. Stir in the malt vinegar, Worcestershire sauce, tomato paste, sugar and a very small amount of salt and pepper. Cool and store in a tightly sealed container.

Sunday Special Eggs Benedict

This special breakfast can be enjoyed as easily at camp as at home.

Yogurt Sauce

¼ cup	light mayonnaise	60 mL
2 tbsp	plain yogurt	30 mL
1 tbsp	Dijon mustard	15 mL
1–2 tsp	fresh lemon juice	5–10 mL
4	eggs	4
4	slices back bacon	4
2	English muffins, halved and toasted	2
1 tbsp	soft margarine or butter	15 mL
	freshly ground pepper	

Serves 2 to 4

Preparation time:
5 minutes

Cooking time:
5 minutes

AT CAMP: In a small bowl, stir together the mayonnaise, yogurt, mustard and lemon juice. In a medium nonstick skillet, add 1 inch (2.5 cm) water; bring to a gentle boil. Slowly slide eggs into water. Poach for 3 minutes or until eggs are cooked as desired. Lift from water to a warm plate to drain. Meanwhile, cook bacon until browned on each side. Place muffin halves on two plates, spreading each with margarine. Top each half with one egg and one slice of bacon. Spoon sauce over the top, then season with pepper and serve.

Cold-Weather Camping

On a winter camping excursion, the weather outside can be stormy, but a fire is cozy and just the solution for making a hot, satisfying meal. Eating well on a winter camping trip makes the effort worthwhile, not only because your body is craving high-energy food to keep warm, but also because there's something gratifying about cooking up a good meal in freezing temperatures. Just remember liquids can become solid. Plan for that. Pack a quality thermos to keep liquids flowing.

Cold Weather Nutrition

It's a given that you're going to need to consume at least double your normal calorie intake when camping in cold weather. Drudging through deep snow all day or just trying to keep warm in your sleeping bag at night requires a lot of energy. You'll need at least 2 pounds (1 kg) of food per day, per person. Eating a low-fat diet is not a good idea. Indulge in fat.

The fewer steps and less time you take to prepare your food the better, not only because it's too darn cold to be bothering with extensive cooking times, but because the fuel for camp stoves burns off a lot quicker in colder temperatures.

You should try to avoid taking fresh foods such as fruit, vegetables and eggs on a cold-weather trip. There's little worry about them spoiling from the temperature, but they contain water, which will freeze and add weight to your pack. Meals like bacon, chicken fajitas, stews, chili, shepherd's pie, burritos and the like are good options for winter cold-weather camping. Precooking the main meals is also a very good idea. It can reduce water content (and weight) and saves a lot of time in camp. The sun goes down quickly during the winter months.

Sandwiches for the day (PB & J, honey, lunch meat, cheese, chocolate-hazelnut spread) can be made up in the morning and kept in an insulated bag with a thermos of hot water for coffee, tea, soup or hot chocolate. Bagels, English muffins or freshly baked bannock are far better than sliced bread. Snacks that contain fat, like fruitcake, work well, so you're not biting into something frozen solid all the time. Dry treats like shortbread don't freeze and are good choices. Cheese and dried meats should be pre-sliced at home rather than you trying to cut into a frozen chunk. Place a sheet of waxed paper between your sandwiches so they don't become one solid lump.

If you choose to cook on a fire, make sure to dig a depression in the snow first and place a layer of sticks (preferably green ones) down. The snow below the fire will eventually begin to melt and your fire will sink down, so having something underneath will stop the fire from being extinguished by the melting snow.

If it's a camp stove you're cooking on then make sure to use an insulated pad under the stove to stop the snow from melting. An old computer mouse pad works great for this. Also, make good use of the stove's heat reflector and windscreen. A homemade cozy for your pots is an excellent way to conserve heat and save on camp fuel as well. And remember, don't take the lid off the pot every minute or two to see if the water is boiling. The old saying is true: a watched pot never boils.

Pressurized gas, especially butane and propane, do not work very well in cold temperatures. Alcohol stoves also have a problem in cold temperatures. Placing the fuel canister in your jacket, even under your armpit, for a short while will help. Alcohol stoves, like the Trangia model, also come with a winter priming plate that helps warm up the fuel before igniting it. White gas stoves that need priming first are best. Take note, however, that liquid gas can quickly become the same temperature as the air, and you can easily get frostbite if you spill it on your bare skin in freezing temperatures.

You can set up a perfect camp kitchen while cold-weather camping. Use a small packable shovel or your snowshoes to dig a 3 foot (1 m) deep trench in the snow. From there you can carve out a table, chairs, storage and cooking area. The area provides shelter from the wind, helping to save fuel in your camp stove.

Dehydration is a major issue when winter camping. You have to remember to drink a lot of liquids throughout the day. If not, it can lead to severe fatigue and contribute to you getting colder, even hypothermic. Problem is, gathering water, not only for drinking but for making meals, is a bit of a challenge. You can melt snow on the campfire or camp stove, but it takes a lot of time and fuel, and the water will have a bland, scorched taste to it. It is possible to decant and aerate the water by pouring the liquid from one bottle into another. Another method to avoid the burned taste is to place at least a half of a cup of water into the pot before adding the snow.

Of course, the problem with that is you'll need a bit of unfrozen water first. Take note as well that placing juice crystals in the water will make it freeze at a lower temperatures than just plain water.

Making a hole through the ice of a nearby lake or river is the better option. A hand-held ice auger can be packed along, but the traditional way is to use an ice chisel. It consists of a heavy-steel chisel blade (beveled on one side is best) with a steel sleeve to fit a long wooden pole into. The wooden pole is held in place by a screw through the sleeve and into the wood. Start chiseling from the outside and work your way in, moving around in a full circle. It's an efficient way to cut a hole in the ice. Also, if you have time and it's one of those sunny late winter days, place a black tarp out in the open, create a depression in the center and place a layer of snow in it. The sun should melt the snow in a couple of hours.

A thermos is best to store water in while traveling, rather than a common plastic bottle. If you do have a water bottle, then use an insulated bottle holder. To keep your water from freezing at night, store the thermos with you inside your sleeping bag or place it upside down in a snowbank so that if the water does begin to freeze, the frozen portion will be at the bottom of the container (and you can still use the liquid on top). The snow should insulate the bottle enough to keep the water from freezing solid, however. Just make sure to mark the spot where you've buried your water.

Try not to drink too much alcohol or caffeine. Alcohol increases your blood flow and cools your core temperature. Caffeine restricts your blood flow and cools your extremities.

Breakfast Cornbread

Cooking up cornbread in a Dutch oven while sipping on morning coffee and stoking the wood stove inside a cozy canvas tent has to be one of the greatest moments while winter camping. Of course, you might have to substitute the pancake syrup with some dark rum if the cold temperature freezes the syrup.

Serves 4

Preparation time:
15 minutes

Cooking time:
40 minutes

2 tbsp	granulated sugar	30 mL
¼ tsp	each ground ginger, cinnamon and nutmeg	1 mL
2 cups	milk	500 mL
¼ cup	cornmeal	60 mL
1½ tsp	canola oil	7 mL
1	egg	1
¼ cup	pancake syrup	60 mL

AT HOME: Combine sugar, ginger, cinnamon and nutmeg; store in a small sealed plastic bag.

AT CAMP: Heat milk in a saucepan. Stir in the cornmeal; reduce heat and simmer, stirring frequently until thickened. Remove from heat, combine oil and egg, stir into cornmeal mixture. Add sugar and spice mixture and syrup, spoon into an 8-inch (20 cm) lightly greased metal pan. Place in the Dutch oven (see page 55). Cook for 40 minutes or until bread is lightly browned and firm to the touch.

CAMP TIP: This bread will need to be cooked with coals both on top of and under the Dutch oven.

Cowboy Breakfast

Pulling all your gear on a freighter toboggan can be a great advantage when winter camping, especially since there's room for your Dutch oven. Of course, you're going to need a good hearty breakfast to pull the toboggan through the deep snow all day, and this one should do the trick.

1	rolled dried sausage, diced	1
½ cup	chopped onion	125 mL
½	sweet red pepper, chopped	½
6	eggs, beaten	0
¼ cup	milk	60 mL
	salt and pepper to taste	
4–6	slices Cheddar cheese	4–6

Serves 4

Preparation time:
10 minutes

Cooking time:
15 minutes

AT CAMP: In a metal pan, cook the sausage, onion and red pepper in a Dutch oven for 10 minutes (see page 55). Combine beaten eggs and milk, pour over sausage, and add salt and pepper to taste. Place cheese on top and cook over coals; no coals are needed on top of the Dutch oven.

Kevin's Blueberry Coffee Cake

This is another of Kevin's favorite winter camping desserts.

1¼ cups	granulated sugar, divided	300 mL
½ cup	shortening	125 mL
½ cup	water	125 mL
1	egg	1
½ cup	all-purpose flour	125 mL
2 tsp	baking powder	10 mL
¼ tsp	salt	1 mL
½ cup	milk	125 mL
2 cups	frozen blueberries	500 mL
½ cup	all-purpose flour	125 mL
½ tsp	ground cinnamon	2 mL
¼ cup	soft margarine or butter	60 mL

AT HOME: Combine ¾ cup (175 mL) sugar with shortening, store in a small plastic bag. In second bag, combine ½ cup (125 mL) flour, baking powder and salt. In third bag, combine ½ cup (125 mL) sugar, flour, cinnamon and margarine to resemble coarse crumbs.

AT CAMP: Place shortening mixture in a large bowl. Stir in water and egg. Beat until mixture is fluffy. In a separate bowl, place the flour, baking powder and salt mixture. Stir in the milk and blueberries until well-mixed; the batter will be thick. Spread batter in a lightly greased deep-dish skillet to bake either in an outback oven or a Dutch oven (see page 55). Sprinkle over batter the contents of the third bag. Bake cake for 20 minutes in the outback oven or 40 minutes in the Dutch oven, or until topping is golden brown.

Mexican Shepherd's Pie

Nancy Chapman, one of Kevin's camping buddies, has provided this recipe for us. She adds about one cup cheese to spread on top of the meat mixture.

1½ lb	cooked ground beef	750 g
1	can (14 oz./398 mL) kidney beans, drained	1
1 cup	corn, frozen or canned	250 mL
1 cup	salsa	250 mL
1	package (35 g) chili seasoning mix	1
1 tbsp	powdered milk	15 mL
3–4 tbsp	ketchup	45–60 mL
1 cup	grated Cheddar cheese	250 mL
1	package instant mashed potatoes	
	paprika	

AT HOME: Combine beef, kidney beans, corn, salsa and chili mix, then dehydrate (see page 65). Store in a tightly sealed container to take to camp.

AT CAMP: In a large bowl, rehydrate the meat mixture with enough water to cover; check periodically for how the mixture is absorbing water, adding extra water if needed to keep covered. Allow to stand for about 30 minutes while setting up camp. That leaves enough moisture to boil without meat becoming too dry. Add powdered milk and ketchup to meat mixture (do not drain off water). Place mixture in a heavy saucepan and bring to a gentle boil until meat mixture starts to thicken. Remove from heat and sprinkle cheese on top. Spread prepared instant mashed potatoes on top of cheese, sprinkle with paprika, and bake in a Dutch oven (see page 55) for 30 minutes or until bubbling and cheese is melted.

Simple Cinnamon Rolls

This is another favorite winter dessert from Kevin. For rolling out the dough, Kevin suggests using the bottom of your freight toboggan.

3 cups	packaged biscuit mix	750 mL
¼ cup	water	60 mL
3 tbsp	soft margarine or butter	45 mL
½ cup	brown sugar	125 mL
¼ cup	raisins	60 mL
1 tbsp	ground cinnamon	15 mL
1 tbsp	canola or olive oil	15 mL
	flour	

AT CAMP: In a medium bowl, combine biscuit mix and water to form a soft dough. Roll out on a floured flat surface. Spread margarine over the surface (a paddle works well) and sprinkle with brown sugar, raisins and cinnamon. Roll into a log and slice into 1 inch (2.5 cm) thick slices, then place into an oiled skillet. Cover pan and bake over low heat for 7 to 8 minutes.

Sourdough Flippers

Kevin has made this dessert many times while winter camping. It is always a success with fellow campers.

Sourdough Starter

2 cups	all-purpose flour	500 mL	Makes 4-6 pancakes
2 cups	lukewarm water	500 mL	**Preparation time:**
1	package dry yeast	1	15 minutes
1	egg or powdered egg equivalent	1	
2 tbsp	granulated sugar	30 mL	**Cooking time:**
½ tsp	salt	2 mL	10 minutes
1 tbsp	canola or olive oil	15 mL	
1 tsp	baking soda	5 mL	
1 tbsp	warm water	15 mL	

AT CAMP: Sourdough Starter: In a large bowl, combine flour, lukewarm water and yeast; allow to stand overnight in a warm place. Next morning the mixture should have risen (even bubbling) and greet you with a fresh yeast aroma. In a large pot or bowl, mix sourdough starter with egg, sugar, salt and oil. Set batter aside for a few minutes. In a small bowl, stir baking soda into warm water. Slowly pour into prepared batter, making sure not to beat it. It will then start to bubble, foam and rise. Let this continue for a minute or two before starting to fry pancakes on a heated, lightly greased griddle. Cook pancakes for a couple of minutes on each side or until bubbles break on top and underside is golden brown; turn and cook other side until golden.

CAMP TIP: It's important to note that baking soda mixture is only added to pancake batter just before you're ready to cook up pancakes.

Thanksgiving in a Pot

Heather Adams, a camping buddy of Kevin's who provided this recipe, gives the following tips: this is a filling, comfort-food style meal for a chilly evening at camp. The quantities for the "Thanksgiving" meal are dependent upon your group size. The serving quantities are always indicated on the packets/boxes but will vary depending on the brand. The additional ingredients (milk, butter, etc.) will also use different quantities, again, based on what the packets/box mixes require. For example, some mashed potatoes call for a lot of milk and butter, some just want a touch of butter and water instead of milk.

Serves 4

Preparation time:
30 minutes

Cooking time:
30 minutes

1	can turkey or chicken	1
1	package gravy mix	1
2 cups	instant mashed potatoes	500 mL
1	box bread stuffing	1
½ cup	toasted walnuts or pecans (optional)	125 mL
	cranberry sauce	

Prepare each ingredient separately. Assemble prepared ingredients as a casserole in layers in a Dutch oven (see page 55) to heat, or set out each separately for folks to assemble themselves (meal will stay warmer if assembled as a casserole, but requires a large pot to do so).

Trail Bars

Kielyn Marrone from Lure of the North Outfitters, another of Kevin's friends to kindly provide a fine recipe, tells us this wholesome trail treat will fill your sweet tooth, while still providing long-lasting nutrition to carry you through a long day on the ice. They are great for winter because their very low water content leaves them soft and chewy well below freezing. Feel free to experiment — use peanuts rather than sunflower seeds, rye flakes for barley, and so on. Enjoy!

1½ cups	barley flakes	375 mL	Makes 12 squares
1¼ cups	large-flake rolled oats	300 mL	
1 cup	smooth almond butter	250 mL	**Preparation time:**
½ cup	rice syrup	125 mL	15 minutes
¼ cup	agave syrup	60 mL	
½ cup	almonds, chopped	125 mL	
½ cup	dried cranberries	125 mL	
¼ cup	sunflower seeds	60 mL	
¼ cup	sesame seeds	60 mL	
1 tsp	vanilla extract	5 mL	

AT HOME: In a large bowl, stir together barley flakes, rolled oats, almond butter, rice and agave syrup, almonds, cranberries, sunflower and sesame seeds and vanilla. Stir until well mixed. Press into a large, lightly greased oblong pan. When firm, cut into squares.

Menu Planning & Nutrition

Organizing your meals is a critical part of designing a good trip. Plan around five main points: 1) Choose meals that make everyone happy. 2) Consider how much food you're packing versus how heavy it is to carry it. 3) Offer variety in recipes. 4) Meet nutritional requirements. 5) Meals, especially dinner, should have a bit of dazzle to them.

Nutrition

Food is what fuels you. To keep it simple, just make sure you give attention to all three main nutrient categories: caloric requirements, carbohydrates and protein.

Calorie intake is essential to allow your body to maintain energy and heat. That's why a camping trip is no time to go on a diet. There's a reason why being outdoors stimulates a good appetite. Your body is craving to be refueled.

The quantity of food to take is still one of the most confusing elements of menu planning, especially if you plan on an interior camping trip where everything is carried on your back. You have so many variables to consider, like the size of the group, eating habits of each individual, the length and difficulty of the trip. The average adult needs 2,500 to 3,000 calories or 1½ to 2 pounds (750 g to 1 kg) of food per day. During strenuous activity the body needs 3,000 to 3,700 calories or 2¼ to 2½ pounds (1.13–1.25 kg) of food per day.

Protein intake is critical because it's what the body uses to keep the engine running. It also helps to build muscle. Protein consists of amino acids in various combinations, and for many people this is done by eating meat. The problem is, keeping meat fresh after a few days is next to impossible, not to mention bulky to carry. However, there's a wide variety of protein substitutes available: nuts, seeds, legumes (peas, various beans and peanut butter), TVP (textured vegetable protein), cheese, powdered milk, powdered eggs and freshly caught fish. In fact, being a vegetarian cook is a huge bonus when it comes to good camp meals.

Carbohydrates are the last key ingredient. Carbs are usually the basis of your meals and provide energy and vitamins to your body. They also fill you up. Some products provide both protein and carbohydrates, like grains, legumes, nuts and seeds. Wheat has the highest protein value, followed by rye and oats. Grits are perfect to have on a trip, whether you eat it as a cereal for breakfast with nuts and honey or as a side dish with dinner with cheese or gravy. Just like bread, brown rice holds more protein then white. Cooking time, however, is much longer. Pasta wins over all the rest as a main carb. It comes in a variety of shapes and sizes, filling the belly and creating some amazing recipe ideas.

Multivitamins

Multivitamins are a good thing to pack along when your trip exceeds eight or nine days. Prior to that time your body should be fine.

To make sure you're getting the proper amount of nutrients while out, one can just check the nutrient labels on each ingredient package and do some math to figure out the grand total per meal. An easier way, however, is to just make sure you have the three key components — calories, protein and carbohydrates — in each main meal.

To get a variety of recipes for meals and snacks, there are many great options in this book. The 7-day menu here is a selection from them. Camp recipes don't have to be found in camp books. Any recipe will do as long as you can keep the ingredients fresh or dehydrate them when packing for the interior.

7-Day Menu

Day 1

Dinner

Snappy Red Pepper Dip, page 103
Butter Chicken with Cabbage, page 107
Encore Potatoes, page 108
Fresh green salad with olive oil and
balsamic vinegar dressing
Banana Brulée, page 125
Tea or coffee, and a chilled white wine
to celebrate the successful setting up of
camp

Day 2

Breakfast

Berry Good Pancakes, page 71. Serve with
maple syrup. Double the recipe for next
day's lunch
Coffee

Lunch

Mushroom Quinoa Salad, page 83
Cold cuts, raw veggies
Fresh milk
Fresh fruit and Hearty Rolled Oat Cookies,
page 97

Dinner

Herb and Garlic Pasta, page 117
Blueberry Coffee Cake, page 166
Cappuccino Creme, page 142

Snacks

Apricot Sunflower Seed Bars, page 92
Cold water or lemonade

Day 3

Breakfast

Cranberry juice
Granola Squares, page 72
Camp-Style Pain au Chocolate, page 68
Coffee

Lunch

Leftover Berry Good Pancakes, page 71
served with extra berries sandwiched
between 2 pancakes
Sun Tea, page 137

Dinner

Corn 'n' Black Bean Salsa, page 95 with
nacho chips
Country Chili, page 108
Cooked brown rice and assorted chopped
fresh vegetables added: cook extra rice for
next day's lunch
Mocha Mousse Cake, page 128, with
added cinnamon for that Mexican flavor
Sober Sangria, page 135 (or mix it up "not
so sober," as desired)

Snacks

Tex Mex Mix, page 102 and Cajun Roasted
Chickpeas, page 102
Lemonade from a powdered lemonade mix

Day 4

Breakfast
Cinnamon French Toast with syrup, page 68
Crisp cooked bacon
Coffee

Lunch
Borscht in Minutes, page 78
Rice Scrambled Eggs, page 86
Juice or lemonade

Dinner
Lentil Dip, page 99, with tortillas
Herb-stuffed Grilled Fish, page 115
Pan-fried Potatoes and Mushrooms, page 118
OR Barley Risotto with Vegetables, page 106
Canned fruit and Fruit 'n' Fiber Cookies, page 72
Irish Coffee, page 133

Snacks
Creamy Apple Cheese Spread, page 96
Crackers
Sliced apples

Day 5

Breakfast
Family-Style Granola, page 69, served with milk and fresh fruit, if available
Bran Muffins, page 94, margarine and jam
Café au lait

Lunch
Salmon Sandwiches, page 86, made using Basic Bannock, page 93
Assorted dried fruits and any fresh fruit still available
Sun Tea, page 137

Dinner
Nacho, Cheese 'n' Salsa Appetizer, page 101
Margarita Pizza with Beer Crust, page 116 (dehydrated tomatoes work best on Day 5)
Quinoa Tabbouleh, page 84
Fast 'n' Easy Chocolate Mousse, page 126

Snacks
Homemade Energy Bars, page 98
Water, lemonade or milk

Day 6

Breakfast
Fruit juice
Overnight Cheese Casserole, page 74
Cooked sausage
Coffee

Lunch
Cheesy Macaroni, page 79
Apples and dried fruit

Dinner
Chips, pretzels and crackers with cheese
Tuna Egg Noodle Casserole, page 121
Baked Lentils and Brown Rice, page 105
Mocha Mousse Cake, page 128
Coffee

Snacks
Bran Muffins, page 94

Day 7

Breakfast
Hot Multigrain Cereal Mix, page 73, with added dried fruit
Basic Bannock, page 93, with margarine and jam. Add any dried fruit to the batter, serve warm with remaining syrup (if there is any)
Camp Coffee

Lunch
Penne Pesto with Tuna, page 85
Tea, water or lemonade

Dinner
Fish, using Marinade for the Fresh Catch, page 152, or Baked Lentils and Rice, page 105
Potato Pancakes, page 118
Apple Cranberry Crisp, page 124

Snacks
Logan Bread, page 100

16

Living off the Land

There's something satisfying about making use of a variety of wild edibles while on a camping trip. Most of us assume plants growing in the wild are simply weeds and are only consumed in "survival" situations. It's true that knowing how to identify a variety of edible plants and berries may save your life out in the woods one day, but the main reason to make use of them is to add nutrition to your diet while camping — not to mention have some fun and reconnect with your natural surroundings. Besides, where else are you going to get fresh veggies or berries on day 10 of an interior trip? As an added bonus, you can also be guaranteed that wild edibles are of the highest quality and have the highest nutritional content — far better than prepackaged foods.

Remember that some plants and berries growing in the wild are very poisonous. Make sure to bring a guidebook to help you properly identify the species. Also, some that are edible are only safe to consume at a particular stage of growth, and others can be harmful if too much is eaten.

Top Wild Edibles

Arrowroot: This water plant, found across North America, grows along the edges of slow-moving rivers. The tubers at the end of the roots are high in starch and can be eaten raw or added to a stew. They're best picked after midsummer to avoid a bitter taste and can even be dried and pounded into a fine flour.

Birch: It is found in most temperate forests of North America. The inner bark is quite bland but can be cut into strips and used as a substitute for spaghetti noodles. The young leaves can also be dried and made into a soothing tea, which is believed to be a cure for urinary tract infections and kidney stones. Yellow birch roots and young twigs have a strong wintergreen taste (and smell) and make an excellent tea when boiled.

Blackberry: This berry grows across North America in different varieties. The thorny bush and the berry itself look similar to raspberry. A very sweet-tasting berry, it is black in color when mature and red prior to being fully ripe.

Blueberry: This is the preferred berry for most campers. It's located all across North America, including the far north. Huckleberries, which are also edible, are usually found growing alongside it. The berries are ripe around midsummer and can be eaten directly off the plant or used in pies, muffins and pancakes.

Bunchberry: The range is north of California and New Jersey, with the plant preferring to grow along the forest floor of mixed woodland. The berries taste something like a bruised apple. They are also somewhat acidic, so don't overdo it.

Cattail: Another water plant that is found across North America but prefers more stagnant water. The entire plant is edible and is probably the best survival food out there. The young spring shoots are the most palatable and are usually peeled back and eaten raw or chopped and mixed into a salad with cucumbers and tomatoes. Fall roots can be eaten as a salad or a cooked vegetable. The roots also make a great substitute for potatoes in a stew. They can also be dried and made into flour.

Cranberry: The plant, which has a wide range across North America, is found along the shores of lakes and ponds. The berries are traditionally picked after the first frost and made into a tasty sauce.

Dandelion: To some this is just a weed in your yard, but to others it's a food source. All parts of the dandelion are edible: young leaves can be added to a salad, and older leaves (more bitter tasting) can be boiled

in two changes of water and the mid-veins removed. Serve with crisp fried bacon, hard cooked eggs, creamed in soups, or baked with meats. The amount of calcium in one serving of dandelion greens is equal to half a cup of milk. Roots may be sliced and used in salads. Best of all, roots can be roasted and used as a coffee substitute; use 1 teaspoon (5 mL) ground roots per cup. Dried leaves can also be uses to make a tea.

Fireweed: This plant has a prominent purple flower and thrives in areas that have been burned by a forest fire. Every part is edible raw (young leaves, flowers, stem and pith). Collect young spring shoots and cook in a small amount of salted water and serve like asparagus. Blanch shoots in boiling water and serve with French dressing. Shoots can also be peeled and eaten raw. Don't eat too much of this plant though — it also acts as a laxative.

Juniper: The berries make an excellent seasoning when dried or crushed on meat or fish. They can also be ground up for a coffee substitute.

Labrador tea: This is the tea of the North. It's found in sphagnum swamps across the northern United States and Canada. The leaves are dried and boiled. To cut the strong acidic taste, try adding a spoon of brown sugar and a shot of liqueur.

Lamb's quarters (pigweed): The young leaves are picked and boiled (they taste a bit like spinach), and the greens may be strained and cooked lightly in cream or milk thickened with flour. The seeds can be added to cornmeal or into a bannock or

bread mix for extra nutrition. The leaves can also be dried and made into a nice tea.

Milkweed: This plant can be found growing in old farmers' fields across the United States and southern Canada. The young sprouts are cooked and eaten like asparagus. The flower pods can also be cooked and stuffed with rice. The bitter milky sap must be removed by boiling the plant in two or three changes of water.

Raspberry: This is a compound berry, consisting of a tight cluster of smaller berry parts. Most compound berries are edible. This bush plant grows across North America. The plant is thorny (but more like thistles than thorns). The berry is reddish in color and tastes sweet. Best eaten fresh since it doesn't dry well.

Salmonberry: This plant grows in wet, coastal forests. The berry, when mature, is a bright yellow-red color. The taste is moderately sweet. The young shoots are also edible raw.

Sowthistles: The young leaves can be used in salads, and the stalks can be cooked like spinach and added to blander tasting greens.

Spruce tips: The new needle growth at the tip of a black spruce tree makes an exceptional tea when boiled. Pine and balsam fir needles also make an excellent vitamin C–enriched tea. As the needles mature, however, they lose their citrus taste and gain a strong resin tang. They can also be added to cookie and cake mixes, especially shortbread. Spruce tip vinegar salad dressing can be an amazing addition to your meals while camping. Mix ½ cup (125 mL) spruce tips with 1 cup (250 mL) red wine vinegar, 1 cup (250 mL) olive oil and ½ teaspoon (2 mL) peppercorns.

Stinging nettle: This prickly plant gets a bad rap because of its small, numerous hollow stinging hairs on the leaves and stems. However, it makes an excellent food source. The young leaves and shoots have a spinach/cucumber taste and are rich in vitamin A, C, iron, potassium, calcium and manganese. Boiling the plant will remove the chemical that stings. When cooked it makes a good green, tea or soup. It's also used in recipes for polenta and pesto. A good rule of thumb is once they are grown past the knees, the plant is too old to harvest. Once the plant begins to develop flowers and seeds it also develops a grainy crystal called cystolith, which irritates the stomach and urinary tract.

Sumac: This plant resembles a tall bush and grows in disturbed areas like roadsides or the edge of farmers' fields. The leaf is compound, made up of several leaflets. The berries grow in clusters and are reddish and fuzzy to the touch. It's the berry that's edible, and it has a lemony/vinegar taste. The berries are usually crushed in water to make a refreshing, lemonadelike drink.

Tiger lily: The bulbs are edible and may be cooked and used as potatoes.

Violets: Young leaves and flower buds can be eaten raw. Mix with lettuce, tomatoes and shredded carrots. Add a few drops of vinegar for dressing.

Watercress: This is an aquatic/semi-aquatic plant found in fast-flowing streams and belongs to the cabbage family. It's also one of the oldest known edible leaf vegetables. It makes a great salad.

Wild ginger: The rhizome can be eaten raw or dried and ground to be used as a substitute for ginger in recipes. The plant grows in moist, shaded woodlands.

Wild leek: Found all across North America, it prefers deciduous woodlots. The root system is best eaten raw for nutritional value and makes an excellent additive to salads. The onion flavor and odor are so overpowering, however, that you may just want to cook it first.

Wild rose: The petals, buds, young leaves and stalks are edible, but the fruit (rosehip) of the plant is the best part. It can be eaten raw or dried for later use. Only eat the outer shell of the rosehip and not the hairy seed cluster.

Wintergreen: The range is more northerly, beginning in the St. Lawrence and Great Lakes region and to the northern tip of the Mississippi River watershed. The leaves and berries, which remain on the plant throughout the winter months, make a soothing and refreshing tea.

Wood lily: The bulbs are edible and may be boiled in water and prepared like potatoes. Boil in two to three changes of water to reduce the bitter taste. It has a peppery flavor.

Yellow pond lily: Yellow pond lily is an aquatic plant usually found in slightly moving water, whereas white water lily is found in stagnant water. The rootstocks are very starchy and can be eaten as a substitute for a potato. Peel, slice, dry and boil in water until tender. The seeds of the yellow pond lily may be dried to loosen the kernels and then lightly ground to remove the shells. With further drying they will swell like popcorn but will not burst. They are very good when lightly salted and served with cream.

Fresh Fish

Eating fresh fish on any camping trip is a major treat. Of course, always have a backup meal packed in case they're not biting. But if you're lucky enough to catch something, then take note that the sooner you eat it, the better. Fish taste best when they are prepared within hours — or minutes — of catching them.

There are a variety of methods to prepare a fish, but gutting and filleting are the two main preferences. Whichever you choose, make sure not to prepare the fish near camp. Animals, including bears, will be attracted to the scent. If you have to clean a fish at camp, then do it on a slab of rock along the shoreline that can be washed off. A paddle makes an excellent cleaning board. Dispose of the remaining bits well away from camp or far out into the lake or river you are camping on.

When choosing between gutting or filleting, it's best to know the difference in species. When preparing a soft-ray fish (e.g., trout), gutting the fish is the most acceptable, basically because the skin and scales of the fish don't need to be removed (and are quite tasty to eat when cooked). A spiny-ray fish (e.g., bass, walleye, pike) need their scales removed if you're going to gut them, so it's best to fillet the flesh.

Gutting a Fish

Using a sharp (filleting) knife, remove the head of the fish by cutting under the pectoral fin (located just past the gill plate). Cut the other side and the head should fall freely off the body. Next, place the pointed end of your knife into the fish's anus and cut along the belly right up to the bone between the two gill flaps. Remove the entrails from inside the ribcage. Also, run your knife (actually your thumb works best) along the inside of the fish to scrape out the blackened blood vessels along the spine. Give the fish a good rinse, and it's ready to cook. You can bake, fry or grill the fish. Just make sure it's done in the center. The flesh will flake away from the bones when it's done. To remove the bones, take hold of the backbone at the top end of the body and lift it gently away from the cooked flesh.

Filleting a Fish

The idea behind filleting is to remove the flesh from the bone (and skin) prior to cooking. It takes more skill and practice than simply gutting a fish, but it's far more effective for cooking it up in various recipes.

It's important to use a sharp and flexible filleting knife. First step is to remove the head just as if you're gutting the fish. You could also leave the head on as long as you cut the fillet free, from the top of the head to behind the pectoral fin, located just past the gill plate. Next, make an incision along the back on one side of the dorsal (top) fin. The idea here is to keep the incision going, running the knife along the dorsal bones from head to tail. Keep your knife angled toward the bone. If you're doing it right you will feel the blade touching the bone, even scraping along it while you slice the flesh clear. Take note that the boney section of the fish ends before the anal fin (located adjacent to the anus, between the belly and tail). You simply cut straight along this section to separate the fillet away from the body.

The process is then repeated on the other side of the fish. This side is more difficult, and you'll often remove less flesh if you don't practice enough. The final step is to remove the fillet from the skin. Place the fillet skin down on a hard surface. Hold the tail end and run your filleting knife along, slicing between the skin and the flesh. Work the knife back and forth, slightly angled toward the skin, and the flesh should easily separate from the skin.

Some Fish Are Bonier Than Others

Pike, for example, have another row of bones (called a Y-bone) running along the backbone. You need to remove this after doing the initial fillet. Place the fillet skin-side down. Locate the row of bones on the fillet by feeling them with your finger. Then, place your knife's edge behind and slice alongside and underneath, making sure to turn your blade upward to keep close to the bone and not waste any meat.

Photo Credits

Cover © Kevin Callan

© Kevin Callan:
Pages 8, 9, 10, 13, 18, 25, 26, 27, 29, 33, 34, 37, 40, 42, 43, 47, 48, 49, 50, 51, 52, 54, 56, 57, 59, 65, 67, 70, 76, 78, 90, 95, 104, 122, 126, 129, 130, 156, 162, 163, 168, 172, 178, 180, 181, 182, 183, 184, 185

© Marc van Vuren / Shutterstock.com:
Page 14

© Ferenz / Shutterstock.com:
Page 19

© Elena Moiseeva / Shutterstock.com:
Page 20

© David S. Baker / Shutterstock.com:
Page 21

© Evgenia Bolyukh / Shutterstock.com:
Page 23

© Mat Hayward / Shutterstock.com:
Page 31

© Timothy Epp / Shutterstock.com:
Page 35

© Margaret Howard:
Page 38

© Lijuan Guo / Shutterstock.com:
Page 44

© Artography / Shutterstock.com:
Page 61

© Marie C. Fields / Shutterstock.com:
Page 63

© Val Thoermer / Shutterstock.com:
Page 138

© Danny Xu / Shutterstock.com:
Page 158

Index